We Are Seven

Caroline Birley

Nabu Public Domain Reprints:

You are holding a reproduction of an original work published before 1923 that is in the public domain in the United States of America, and possibly other countries. You may freely copy and distribute this work as no entity (individual or corporate) has a copyright on the body of the work. This book may contain prior copyright references, and library stamps (as most of these works were scanned from library copies). These have been scanned and retained as part of the historical artifact.

This book may have occasional imperfections such as missing or blurred pages, poor pictures, errant marks, etc. that were either part of the original artifact, or were introduced by the scanning process. We believe this work is culturally important, and despite the imperfections, have elected to bring it back into print as part of our continuing commitment to the preservation of printed works worldwide. We appreciate your understanding of the imperfections in the preservation process, and hope you enjoy this valuable book.

We Are Seven

Caroline Birley

Nabu Public Domain Reprints:

You are holding a reproduction of an original work published before 1923 that is in the public domain in the United States of America, and possibly other countries. You may freely copy and distribute this work as no entity (individual or corporate) has a copyright on the body of the work. This book may contain prior copyright references, and library stamps (as most of these works were scanned from library copies). These have been scanned and retained as part of the historical artifact.

This book may have occasional imperfections such as missing or blurred pages, poor pictures, errant marks, etc. that were either part of the original artifact, or were introduced by the scanning process. We believe this work is culturally important, and despite the imperfections, have elected to bring it back into print as part of our continuing commitment to the preservation of printed works worldwide. We appreciate your understanding of the imperfections in the preservation process, and hope you enjoy this valuable book.

"BIRDIE'S DEAREST TREASURES"

Chap. I

WE ARE SEVEN.

A Tale for Children.

BY

CAROLINE BIRLEY.

WITH

COLOURED ILLUSTRATIONS BY T. PYM.

London:
WELLS GARDNER, DARTON, & CO.
PATERNOSTER BUILDINGS.

CONTENTS.

CHAP.		PAGE
I. MISS JUDY	. . . .	1
II. TABLEAUX	. . . . . .	17
III. DOLLY'S MISSION	. . . . .	36
IV. A BIRD OF PASSAGE	. . . .	62
V. DIFFICULTIES	. . . . .	79
VI. BABYLAND	. . . . . .	94
VII. THE SECOND MRS. ENDERBY	. . .	110

WE ARE SEVEN.

CHAPTER I.

MISS JUDY.

> "An earnest child,
> Now looking straight at you, now laughing wild."
> —Leigh Hunt.

ONCE upon a time the bright June sunshine lighted up the pretty gardens which surrounded Woodlands, a large white-washed and gabled house, belonging to Colonel Enderby, who, having left the army many years ago, had come back to the village which was his birthplace, and which he well remembered as a little boy.

The place was not much altered. Although three

or four miles off, the great manufacturing town of Milborough smoked and blackened the atmosphere a little more with its tall chimneys, and a couple of factories or dyeworks established in the valley increased and gave employment to the Norrington inhabitants, that small village, with its long and level High Street and sloping rows of cottages on the hillside, was just the same as ever, and there, among fields and flowers, the children led an active, healthy, outdoor life, which seemed like a repetition of their father and Aunt Dolly's early days.

Thus passed six happy years, and then came sorrow: Alan, the youngest child, a bright little fellow of eighteen months, died suddenly of croup, and in a few short weeks his mother, who had long been delicate, followed him to the pretty churchyard, which was only separated from the Woodlands garden by a narrow lane. The children used often to find their way there, and on certain special occasions—Easter, or Christmas, or birthdays—hung lovely garlands on the cross which formed the headstone of the grave: at Judith's earnest request, the plants and flowers upon it were left entirely in their charge, and bloomed freshly and brightly in due season.

Judy and her brother Geoffrey were old enough then

to retain a distinct recollection of that mournful time, but to the others it was like a painful dream, and they did not often pause to think of what had happened in the early ages of two years and a half ago. Little Barbara—or Birdie, as they called her—used to talk of baby Alan, and fancy she remembered him, but this was merely a habit learnt from Judith, and neither she nor Rory nor the twins could realise a different life from that they led at present, with the daily governess, Miss Gresley, to teach the girls, and three old servants —Rogers the gardener, Giles the butler, Elizabeth the nurse—to spoil and scold them all alike. People who pitied Colonel Enderby for his charge of those rough children, would have been surprised to find how much their sympathy was wasted: he could work unmoved amid a noise and chatter which would have driven most men to distraction, and lightly regarded the complaints which the long-suffering domestics sometimes brought him in the holidays—such as that Master Rory and Miss Judy had been riding their old ponies at the cows in the big field (chasing wild buffaloes on the prairie, *they* called it), until there wasn't a drop of milk for tea; or that, in Rogers' dinner-hour, the jargonelle pear-tree had been stripped of the fruit which he was saving for dessert. The Colonel had been a boy himself, and had indulged in similar exploits of his own: he did not mind that sort of thing, so long as his half-dozen grew up brave and frank and loyal, but the least approach to meanness or deceit was visited with a cold displeasure which was very hard to bear, and the offender would have gone through almost anything to be restored to favour. Strangers thought him rather stern, but then they did not see him in his home.

The shrubs were in their summer glory: great clumps of rhododendron bushes were now one mass of purple blossom, lilacs and Guelder roses flourished in the borders, yellow laburnums hung in graceful sprays, and although geraniums and petunias were scarcely yet in flower, their foliage covered up the bareness of the beds upon the lawn. As the clock in the stable-tower struck the hour of five, two well-grown boys of twelve and fifteen came racing up the avenue, and at the welcome sound a head of auburn hair emerged from the middle of a big hawthorn tree, and their eldest sister, Judy, swung herself lightly to the ground. A pile of lesson-books, which she had balanced on an upper bough, followed her descent in a sort of little shower, but before she picked them up she ran a few steps to the house, and, pausing, whistled in shrill, clear notes an imitation of a bugle call.

The summons reached the pleasant-looking school-room, where a bonny little damsel of eight years old, with long brown hair hanging down her back, was busy piling up the slates in a corner, putting away the shabby globe under the piano, and collecting the many pens and copy-books and bits of pencil which were strewn about the room; while her double and twin sister Dolly tried gently to persuade a very tiny little girl, who was curled up in an arm-chair near the window, to learn her lesson properly instead of gazing at the waving trees outside. At the well-known signal, which with her poetry unlearnt she was not able to obey, Birdie's brown eyes filled with tears, and Dolly, hastily promising to come back to her directly, ran off quickly with Dulcie down the stairs, and found Judith and her brothers waiting on the lawn.

Birdie heard their merry voices down below, and felt solitary and ill-used; she ran to the window, but she could not see them, and perhaps they were forgetting that she was the point of the meeting, and that it was the keeping of *her* birthday on the 2d of July that they had to consider. Birthdays were always great festivals in the Enderby family, each child in turn choosing some special treat, and the plan had to be submitted to their father for approval a long time before the day. This year, Birdie and Judith had quite made up their minds: the other four had simply to hear and to obey.

Birdie hoped that it would prove a very grand affair. It was nicer to think of that than to attend to her lesson, especially as she could not now expect to learn it in time to join the others before tea; so she tucked herself up again in the big chair and went off into another day-dream. What a large party they would be, with Uncle Harry and Aunt Dolly coming for a visit, and then it was such a happy chance that Geoff and Rory were at home! They ought properly to have been at Winchester, but all the young Enderbys had been ill that spring with scarlatina and had just come back from the seaside. Although the danger of infection was quite over, the school authorities had decided not to receive the boys until after the Midsummer holidays; and in order not to waste their time entirely, they used to go down to the village each afternoon but Saturday, to study for a couple of hours with the curate, Mr. Martindale. It was rather a grievance that he could not take them in the mornings on account of parish work, but Geoffrey, who was bent upon treading in his father's footsteps and entering the Royal Engineers, understood the necessity of preparing for his examinations, and Rory was generally happy in following his example.

"Do you know your lessons, twins?" asked Judith with authority, as the younger ones came out. "Were you ready to come down?"

"Oh yes! they were quite easy," Dolly answered; "but yours looked such hard ones. You have been very quick."

"Ah! but I haven't finished," said Miss Judy. "My Latin for father I have never touched. I shall learn it in bed to-morrow. You know I can always awake early if I like."

"Dolly, take my books upstairs," said Geoffrey. "You shall have a tithe of my sweets next time we buy some."

Dolly nodded at the accustomed bribery. "All right! Shall I take yours, Judy?"

"You may as well," said Judy, bundling them hastily into her little sister's arms. "Just shake the tree, Rory! Ollendorf is missing, and I know it was up there."

Roderick, a merry, fair-haired boy, obeyed, and the unlucky book came tumbling to the ground, and was thrown across the grass to Dulcie, who caught it deftly in her ready hands.

"Where's Birdie?" Judith asked. "What a time she is! isn't she coming? we can't begin without her."

"Not yet," said Dulcie seriously. "She says her poetry is so difficult that she shall never know it; and she was going to cry a little bit, I think."

"And you left her!" Judith said, with flashing eyes. "You horrid, heartless children! No, Dolly, thank you; I can carry my books myself. You needn't wait for me; I daresay I shall be some little time."

"But, Judy," began Dulcie, anxious to explain on her sister's behalf that Dolly had promised to go back and help her; but impetuous Judy would not wait, and rushed upstairs in her peculiar fashion, one step, two steps at a time.

"The meeting is dissolved," said Geoffrey solemnly. "Parliament is prorogued; the members disperse for their autumn holiday somewhat earlier than was anticipated. Dulcie, I want the old red rug to lie on; and, while you are about it, just bring a shawl to make a pillow for my head. And, Doll, you fetch me 'Ivanhoe;' it is in my room, or on the landing, or perhaps I left it in the hayloft."

"And I shall go and look at Trojan's pups," said Rory, sure that his admiring sisters would follow him when Geoff's commands had been obeyed. He was very fond of animals, and this hideous black-and-white bull-terrier was the delight and darling of his heart.

Meanwhile, Miss Judy was in the schoolroom. She was a bright, clever girl, high-principled, generous, determined, and had great power and influence over her brothers and sisters. If any of the six were in disgrace, she was the first to take the blame, and was always ready to give up her rights in favour of a younger one; but, in return, she had a great desire to stand first in their affections. She was Geoffrey's favourite sister, his 'Miss Judy,' Birdie was her darling, little Alan used to love her best of all, but Roderick and the twins had an unpleasant knack of perfect happiness without her, which poor Judith did not like; and although nothing would have given her greater pleasure than the belief that the father, who trusted her entirely, loved her a little better than his other children, he never in any way made favourites, while their old nurse Elizabeth, who, with unwearied care looked after their health and physical well-being, showed a decided preference for Barbara and Rory.

Geoff, who was older than Judith, asserted his equality by a good deal of amicable teasing and a little real annoyance at her tomboy ways; but, like all the others, he generally submitted to her wishes, and he and she were special friends. In appearance they were a striking contrast: Geoff, a singularly good-looking and well-mannered boy, having inherited his father's clear-cut features and grave look; while Judy's freckled face and turn-up nose resembled no one in particular, and she scarcely ever for two minutes looked the same. Time would probably improve her, but at fourteen she was a plain girl, slight and very tall, and with an honest, thoughtful look in her grey eyes. She had quantities of wavy, auburn hair, which was always plaited upon great occasions, though she preferred wearing it in a flowing mane. Her garden frocks were generally dirty, her boots unbuttoned or unlaced, and her necktie fastened anywhere but underneath her chin. Indeed, her untidiness seemed hopeless, and though for the sake of pleasing her aunt Dolly, Mrs. Lennox, Judy sometimes made a short-lived effort, she had a private theory that her want of beauty made personal adornment an utter waste of time.

"You idle child! why don't you learn your lesson?"

Little Barbara looked up brightly at the kindly greeting, and, as her sister knelt beside her, hid her face for an instant upon Judy's shoulder.

"Oh, my Judy! it is so difficult," she murmured plaintively, but with a roguish smile of contradiction in her eyes.

It was such an odd little face, very thin and brown and small, and Birdie, when she talked, had a trick of wrinkling her nose and forehead and screwing up her eyes, which gave a very comical effect. There was just a look of Judith in the variety and intelligence of expression, but Birdie was much prettier, and her dark-brown eyes were almost unnaturally large and bright. Sea breezes had failed to bring back her strength after the scarlatina, and, always more delicate than the others, she now seemed more easily tired. Everybody spoilt her, she was so bright and winning, and Judy's rough, imperious tones and boyish gestures always softened strangely beneath the touch of Birdie's little arms. Ever since their mother's death, Judith had striven not to let her miss the sweet caressing ways to which she had been used.

The lesson was not a hard one,—two new verses of Wordsworth's ballad, "We are Seven," to learn by heart, and some of the old to look over for repetition. To a child of Birdie's quickness it was nothing, but being in an idle mood and always very readily affected by melancholy things, the poem had taken a strong hold of her imagination. Do you know the story of the poet who, talking with a little country girl, asks the number of her brothers and sisters, and she tells him they are seven in all,—two in Conway, two at sea, while two are lying in the green churchyard so near the cottage door where she is living with her mother?

> "If two are in the churchyard laid,
>   Then ye are only five,"

he answers in his grown-up wisdom, but with gentle firmness she refuses the correction.

> "Still
> The little maid would have her will,
>   And said, 'Nay, we are seven.'"

"Two verses have you, Chick?" said Judy. "We will learn them together. I will read it first, and you shall say it after me—

> 'So in the churchyard she was laid;
>   And all the summer dry
> Together round her grave we played,
>   My brother John and I.'

Now, Birdie!" and thus the lesson went on until the lines—

> "My brother John was forced to go,
>   And he lies by her side."

And then Birdie, whose voice had been growing very

shaky and unsteady, broke down altogether, and she said with a little sob—

"Judy, I can't say it! I counted us, and we are seven too, and it makes me think of Alan and want him back again. I read it all, and the little girl doesn't seem to mind, but *I* do; and then I nearly cried, and Dolly said she would come back and tell me all about it."

"The little girl was a duffer," said Judith.—"Oh, I forgot that father said I wasn't to talk more slang than I could help.—Anyway, I don't think she was clever; you know it says she was 'a simple child.' And yet, Birdie, perhaps she was right. When people ask us how many we are, I always hate it; I never know what to say. It seems so unkind to leave out Alan, just because he can never play with us, and yet he isn't exactly one of us any more. But, then, there is what we say in church."

"What is that?" said Birdie.

"I believe in the Communion of Saints," repeated Judith, looking straight before her. "I can't explain exactly what it means, although I think I understand, but I suppose that if we didn't believe we shouldn't put any more flowers upon mother and Alan's grave, and should just try to forget them as quickly as we could.

Yes, we are seven, little Birdie, although one of us is lying over there."

"I shall *never* be ready to go out," said Birdie in despair.

Judy turned resolutely to the book again, "Suppose we teach it to your boys! Where are they now?" she said.

"Dulcie took them to the library to change their books, and they haven't come back yet," was the grave answer; and Miss Judy, understanding, walked straight up to the bookcase and brought out from a half-filled shelf Birdie's dearest treasures, the four large ninepins which she called her "boys." She was a devoted mother, who, with true maternal instinct, failed to see that the loveliest china, wax, or composition dolls had qualities superior to those of her own children, and indeed she steadily refused to play with them—a very nice big china one called Laura, which had been given to her, being rather a trouble until she hit upon the brilliant plan of sending her to a boarding-school in Germany, which, as the distance was too great for her to come home for the holidays, accounted for her perpetual residence at the bottom of a seldom-opened drawer.

The boys were most convenient: you could knock them about, or wash them, or put them near the fire without much risk to life or limb; and although it was a little awkward that they had no arms to hold with or be held by, and were physically incapable of sitting down, these deficiencies were fully atoned for by the erect carriage of their tall and slender figures and their power of standing steadily upright. Their style of dress was simple, consisting merely of a sort of smock or waggoner's frock, generally of sarsenet, tied round the waist with a sash: Richard's was dark reddish brown, Walter's white with light-blue ribbon, while James and Frank, the little ones, wore cherry-coloured garments, the elder being distinguished from his brother by a black velvet band. Few things wounded Barbara's feelings so much as to allude to them as ninepins, but once a far more terrible calamity occurred: the four had been undressed and carefully arranged according to their ages when the child was called away, and in the meantime the maid coming in to lay the cloth for tea mixed them up together and put them on the piano in a little heap. Birdie shed bitter tears. To know them again was impossible; they were exactly similar in size, height, and complexion, and "as like as four ninepins" passed into a proverb, which the real boys were apt to quote. Miss Judy was employed to draw rude faces in pen and ink upon the smooth, round heads, so that the mistake might never be repeated, but the mother still had qualms, lest in reality her bright, high-principled Richard was being punished for the childish naughtiness of little Frank, or clever, studious Walter masqueraded with the brilliant robes, unquenchable spirits, and turbulent disposition of idle Master James.

Birdie's face lighted up directly as Judith placed the class before her, and the lesson began in earnest. The child's heart was in it now, her thoughts distracted from the grievance of learning all alone, and when in a little time Judy suddenly exclaimed, "I believe Walter can say it now!" Birdie, in his person, repeated it with perfect ease, and was carried off in triumph to the garden swing. At six o'clock the tea-bell rang, which brought in the whole party, and the birthday discussion then began, Judith being as usual the chief speaker.

CHAPTER II.

TABLEAUX.

"Great is the joy when leave is won,
On sun-bright holiday,
To deck some passive little one
In fancy garments gay:
Whether it be a bright-haired boy,
With brow so bold and high,
Or maiden elf with aspect coy,
Grave lip, and laughing eye."
—*Lyra Innocentium.*

"YOU see," said Miss Judy, planting her elbows on the table, and looking round at the assembled company, "it is rather a poser to find something that will suit us all. Elizabeth declares that Birdie isn't strong enough for a regular outing, which knocks off picnics and excursions and all that kind of thing, and though we thought of a tremendous supper in the hayloft, that would, after all, be better for an autumn or a winter birthday, when it wouldn't be so hot for cooking, and we could save up our money for candles. The twins might choose it, and if we can afford it, we might have a big gas star over the doorway, like the one they had at the 'Dog and Partridge' when the Prince of Wales was married."

"Suppose you tell us what we *are* to have, instead of everything that is no good; it is shorter and quite as interesting," said Geoff severely. "Rory, pass the marmalade. And I do wish, Miss Judy, that you wouldn't always put your elbows in the butter."

With a rueful face his sister rubbed her sleeve and put her arms resolutely down. "Well then," she continued, "Birdie said that she should like a party with lots of children, because it is such ages since we have been allowed to have any; and we are going to ask father to let us have supper and a dance—you like dancing, don't you, Geoff? Only when first they come, both the very little ones and the big boys are so slow; they stare at one another and won't speak, and the tiny things cling to their sisters or the nursery-maids, and it is all horrid for a time. And so we thought a little acting to begin with would take off the stiffness, and Aunt Dolly will be here to help, you know."

As she looked round for approbation, Geoff responded,

"All right, old girl," and every one seemed pleased but Rory, who muttered discontentedly that dancing was beastly, and he shouldn't act, for it was such a grind to learn one's part.

Judy shook her head at him, and chanted, laughingly,

"'Nobody asked you, sir,' she said,"

and Birdie looked up with a flush of satisfaction on her little cheeks. "Oh, but nobody will have anything to learn. We are to stand quite still, and make lovely pictures, and not say one single word. And then every one is to guess what we are."

"Tableaux," said Dolly, "that will be nice;" and she gave Birdie's hand a sympathetic little squeeze underneath the table.

"This is to be a sort of acrostic," Judith continued grandly. "You don't know what an acrostic is, Dulcie? no more did I until a few days ago when I saw it in a book, and then father explained. It isn't a riddle, and it isn't a charade,"——

"Or an enigma, or a puzzle, or a rebus, or a problem," finished Geoff; "so now you can tell us what it is."

"It is something you have to guess and spell," said Judy vaguely. "Don't laugh, Geoff. I know what I mean, if you don't. We thought of the word 'Woodlands.' The first picture, therefore, would have to be something beginning with W. (Whittington, for instance), and the second and third would be O's, and the fourth a D, and so on until we spelt the whole word. There will have to be nine tableaux, and father and the others must guess them one by one until they find out what we mean."

"And, Geoffrey, all the pictures are to be fairy tales and nursery rhymes," said Birdie eagerly.

"All right! I'll be Bluebeard, and you girls shall be some of my wives," said Roderick kindly, flourishing the bread knife as he spoke.

"Where is the B in Woodlands, Rory?" asked Dulcie slyly.

"It shall be managed somehow," Judith promised. "Yes, it will do for A, Ann, Sister Ann, you know. She can be standing on the battlements, waving her handkerchief to her brothers, while Bluebeard is in the act of killing Fatima in the courtyard. Only you must have a very blunt knife, Rory; I daren't trust you with a sharp one when you are excited."

"If it is *very* blunt, I will be Fatima," said Dolly. "Here is father! we can ask him at once."

Six pairs of eyes turned towards the doorway, as

the tall soldierly figure walked into the room, and in another moment little Barbara had climbed upon her chair, and was standing with her arms about his neck, presenting her petition in a torrent of quick words.

"Please, please, father darling, do let us have a real big party," she concluded coaxingly, "and I *promise* I will dance with you."

"A crowning inducement," was his answer. "Well, I see no objection, if you can persuade your Aunt Dolly to make the arrangements and to help you with the invitation list—your best handwriting, Judy, mind."

"And only half as many blots as usual," put in Rory.

"Won't you have some tea to-night?" said Judith, "that is, if you are not *very* particular. I had to put in plenty of hot water, for the boys do take so many cups. Geoffrey has had four."

"Aren't you going to dine with me?"

"Yes, it makes no difference," said Geoff, who always had late dinner with his father.

"You see," said Judy good-humouredly, "one hasn't any hold upon them now. Long ago when Mary used to bring up hot water in a jug, she wouldn't answer the bell more than half a dozen times for anything, however much we rung it; but now we have the kettle, the number of cups is quite unlimited. I wish we might keep a tea-caddy too."

"Or a tea-chest," said the Colonel. "Surely, Judy, one may, without being *very* particular, object to the quality of this mild-looking beverage. Is this what she generally gives you, Rory?"

"Can't you drink it, father?"

"My child, I shall not try. What I came to tell you is that I have had a letter from your uncle, who finds that he can get away on Friday and be with us for ten days. Then he goes to Ireland to look out for a house, and while he is putting it in order, your aunt will stay and do the same to us."

"How awfully jolly!" Judith said with sparkling eyes.

"Yes, but now for something melancholy. Miss Gresley has been speaking to me" (Judy looked a little bit alarmed) "and wished to know whether it would be very inconvenient for the holidays to begin on Saturday instead of waiting until the middle of next week. She wants to join her"——

But the end of the sentence was lost in a loud cheer, "Hip hip, hurrah!" and an invitation from Miss Judy to a grand inauguration tea in the beech-tree arbour.

Until her marriage, four years previously, Aunt

Dolly's home had been with her brother, and in her the children found their brightest playmate, best adviser, and safest *confidante*. Their mother was often ill and busy, and could not be disturbed, but *she* had always leisure to attend to them; and great was their consternation and dismay when Major Lennox, whose regiment was stationed at Milborough, triumphantly stepped in and carried off his prize. The brothers-in-law had long been friends, and the younger Dorothea was the Major's godchild. All the children had grown very fond of him in spite of this one grievance, but he made special favourites of the dainty little twins, whose delicate features and neat figures at first sight resembled each other so exactly, that strangers seldom knew the difference between them; though, if you looked closely at the little faces, you could see that the expression upon Dulcie's was shyer and sweeter than her sister's, and that Dolly's firm red lips and big grey eyes had the bright decision and intelligence which invented the numerous schemes they carried out together: her face was also, if anything, the rounder and more rosy of the two.

What a merry, noisy tea that was in the beech-tree arbour! what laughter and fun and chatter! what piles of big red strawberries and jugs of thick, rich cream! what sad regrets from Rory that it was too early in the season for the usual plate of unripe gooseberries from the Lancashire-lad tree, which was the pride and glory of his plot of ground! and what contributions of lettuces, mustard and cress, and radishes from the other little ones! Then how bright and eager was the resentment of their uncle's unkind insinuation, that the professional care of their gardens during their seaside visit had much improved the produce of those beds! How rash and ready and generous the promises of future dishes of carrots, turnips, peas, potatoes, and French beans! How strong the hope which could predict such great results from the tiny shoots of green which in some instances were scarcely visible above the soil! Aunt Dolly noted lovingly the changes in the little flock she had not seen since Christmas. Geoff's handsome face had grown more thoughtful and manly, the twins were taller, Rory's curly head was darker; Judith's manner to the younger ones had a pride and motherliness which touched her, and Birdie—dear little Birdie—had surely not looked quite so delicate before. The child was on her uncle's knee, imploring him to stay until her birthday, and Colonel Enderby seconded her efforts.

"The children are bent upon a grand affair," he said, "and your services as stage-manager are indispensable."

"With Geoff to help, I may feel equal to the post," said Major Lennox. "I know of old his capabilities with a box of tools."

"I suppose we may have a stage to manage then," said Geoff, "or else the post would be a sinecure."

"And Judy and I will undertake the dresses," said Mrs. Lennox mischievously, for the girl's aversion to a needle was well known.

"Not I, indeed!" she was beginning hastily, when Geoffrey interrupted. "Never mind, Miss Judy; when you go to school and I pay that twopence extra for manners that I shall never, never grudge, we will see that the rudiments of plain sewing are not neglected."

"Judy *always* cobbles my boys' frocks," said indignant little Birdie in defence.

"I'm afraid I do," said honest Judith; but the thought of school had brought a cloud upon her brow. In eighteen months she was to go to one at Brighton, and she looked forward to the prospect with unspeakable dismay.

Major Lennox saw the shadow, and called her to him. "Come along, Miss Judy! it is a pity to break up the meeting, but time is short, and you and Geoff must show me where the stage can go. Is the village carpenter a good one?"

And now began a season of great mystery. The schoolroom was wholly given up to preparations for the grand event, and in place of dictionaries and grammars, nothing was seen but the "Child's Own Book of Fairy Tales," the "Treasury of Pleasure-books," Aunt Louisa's shilling series, mutilated copies of "Nursery Rhymes," and similar light literature; and the family theatrical wardrobe produced all sorts of wondrous stores,—muslin scarves embroidered in silver, quilted petticoats more rich in colour than material, flowered waistcoats of a bygone date, a military tunic, flannel suits adorned with ribbons, two or three turbans, scarlet shoes with brilliant buckles, numerous old hats, and a quantity of fuzzy-looking stuff for hair. Here Aunt Dolly and Letty the sewing-maid set to manufacturing pretty, quaint costumes, while Judith, perched upon the table or piano, picked out in her story-book the happiest bit for illustration, and showed a real facility in grouping and arranging the performers. The girl was in her element. Every one treated her as the responsible head, and her sisters besieged her constantly with offers of some special treasure, which the owner used to say, "would look so pretty in a picture," Birdie especially entreating that Jessie-Tibbie-Ruth, her favourite white cat, should frequently appear. Then Birdie didn't know

"RORY LOOKING VERY GRAVE STOOD BEHIND HIS SISTER'S CHAIR, BESTOWING FURTIVE KISSES ON AN UGLY LITTLE MASS OF BLACK AND WHITE"

Chap. II

the stories or had forgotten them, and Judith would go down on the floor with her small child nestling up against her, as she told in flowing language the history of Dick Whittington, Bluebeard, or Dame Trot, until summoned by a shout, "Miss Judy!" to a conference with Geoff, in which the free use of the terms, "wings, greenroom, footlights, call-boy," had a most imposing sound. The boys had a regular carpenter's shop outside, where they worked with a young gardener, and some of Judy's happiest hours were spent in sharing their hard labour: she was nearly as good as Rory in the use of hammer, saw, and plane, and although her fingers suffered greatly in the acquirement of the art, it was a point of honour in the family not to be afraid of pain.

At length the long-expected day arrived, and Barbara, coming down to breakfast, found a heap of presents by her plate—from Geoff, a table for her boys of his own making; from Uncle Harry and Aunt Dolly, a book called "Fairyland;" from Judy, a pearl locket, which had been their mother's, with a tress of auburn hair. The twins presented jointly a pincushion and a needlebook, which they had made together; and Rory, looking very grave, stood behind his sister's chair, bestowing furtive kisses on an ugly little mass of black and white, one of Trojan's cherished puppies which, generous as he was, it nearly broke his heart to give away. His money was all spent, and he had nothing else for which the child would care. "Here you are, Birdie," he said suddenly, putting it on her knee. "I meant to call him 'Pepper,' but you may give him any name you like; only mind you don't let Jessie scratch him, till he's big." After a certain age Trojan's progeny could be trusted to defend themselves.

"That is the widow's mite," said Aunt Dolly to her brother.

"Now, Rory, fetch *my* present," said Colonel Enderby after breakfast, "and we will come to the front door and look;" and in two or three minutes the boy came up the avenue, driving a snow-white little pony in a pretty two-wheeled cart. "For you and Judy together, my little girl," said her father. "Now you will be able to join the others on their expeditions, and perhaps one of them will take you for a drive to-day."

"Oh, I will!" died away on Judy's lips as she noticed Roderick's face, and she promptly changed her sentence. "I daresay Rory can; he's not so busy as we are."

"And you had better go this morning," said his aunt. "Birdie must have a rest before the excitement to-night."

The stage, which stood at one end of the long dining-room with an entrance from the conservatory, by which the actors came, was highly creditable to the efforts of Major Lennox, Geoffrey, and the carpenter. Sixty or seventy spectators were gathered before the curtain, the seniors in the background and in front the rows of children, gradually diminishing in size. Some people thought their bright, expectant faces made the prettiest picture of the whole. Down went the lights, a little bell was heard, and the crimson curtains rolling back revealed—through an open door into the cottage—a woodland path in the far distance with foxgloves growing on each side. A little bed stood in one corner, and, framed in a huge white cotton nightcap, a wolf's head rested on a pillow, with a terrific glare in the glassy-looking eyes. A common chair, with a cup of water, spoon, and medicine bottle upon it, was close at hand, and shyly standing by the open door was a charming little maiden with a scarlet hood upon her light-brown hair. She had a bunch of wildflowers in her hand, and a basket full of cheesecakes hung upon one dimpled arm. Loud was the applause as the drop-scene fell, and twice it rose again; then, sighing with relief, little Barbara sprang away into Judith's waiting arms.

Scene the second displayed a handsome carved oak chair or throne from which rich furs were carelessly depending, and lazily reclining in the midst a small black velvet monarch held his court. Long fair curls fell from under his round cap of scarlet and ermine, between his lips there was a pipe, and a pair of scarlet legs rested on the edge of the stool, where stood a china bowl. His lords (arrayed in mantles not unlike the opera cloaks of the Enderby girls) were grouped about his chair, and to the right of the audience three fiddlers were ready to discourse sweet music. Their little king surveyed them with a merry twinkle in his eyes.

In tableau three, Judith was the chief attraction. Half the stage was taken up by an immense black shoe, out of the top of which peeped several shy and frightened childish heads, some bending discontentedly over the soup basins in their hands, and others too much fascinated by the fate of their companion, a ragged little urchin in shirt sleeves, who, cowering in his mother's grasp, received the punishment of his misdeeds. Over her petticoat of Turkey-red she wore a chintzy bedgown, the muslin cap and apron were snow-white, and a brilliant red-bordered yellow kerchief gave a striking bit of colour: the costume was completed by her powdered hair, high black felt hat, and pair of spectacles. With one hand she grasped her victim by the collar; the other arm uplifted held a formidable birch.

Number four presented a long row of domestics standing at one side, and gazing scornfully at the dirty, shabby-looking boy, who was shedding bitter tears over the large white cat, which, tightly clasped against him, nestled on his breast. A bluff sea-captain held his hand outstretched to take it, and his master, Mr. Fitzwarren, encouraged the poor lad with signs. Beautiful Miss Alice had stolen up to him with eyes of tender pity; and at the end of the performance her arms received from Rory her cherished darling, Jessie-Tibbie-Ruth.

The fifth tableau was in three compartments: the out-door scene occupying the background of the centre, where shocks of corn were strewn about the floor, and large toy lambs and cows feeding in imaginary fields. In front of them and gazing round inquiringly, stood a youthful shepherdess, her dress, all over rosebuds, tucked up above her pretty quilted petticoat of pink, and a hat garlanded with flowers upon her head. She leant a little on her crook, and behind her—rather to the right—Little Boy Blue, in lovely satin garments, lay sleeping by the haystack, a golden horn hanging at his waist. In the next division, little Miss Muffet, in quaint brocaded silk of the last century, shrank away in terror from a tremendous wooden spider, leaving curds and whey to fate; while her companion, in the shape of a self-complacent little sailor, ate up his mince-pie in peace and quietness. This time the applause was more spirited than ever, and in the longer interval Dolly Bo-peep put on her Eastern dress.

A length the curtain rose upon a foreign land, indicated chiefly by the tubs of orange trees, which, recently imported from the conservatory, now blossomed freely in Bluebeard's courtyard, and here Rory, in his uncle's dressing-gown, his fair face almost hidden in a mass of azure wool, threatened the life of pretty Fatima with a dazzling, harmless scimitar. A square turret, constructed of the wall-paper which is made to look like blocks of stone, had a small step-ladder in the middle, on which stood Sister Ann in Chinese dress and splendid turban, waving violently with her handkerchief for help.

Once more the woodland scene, but this time it was night, and on the darkened stage could be seen somewhat dimly the distant groves of trees, though one pale ray of moonlight shone upon a foreground strewn with boughs and leaves. There, their young heads pillowed on a stone, two little children were lying in a close embrace, their scanty garments leaving visible the bare and pretty legs and feet, and the arm of the elder thrown protectingly around the younger, who held a bunch of scarlet berries in his hand. Robin-redbreasts were perched upon the branches, or flying up and down.

In number eight there was but one figure—Dame Trot carrying home her cat; but the old-fashioned kirtle of dark blue and the high mob-cap were so becoming to Aunt Dolly, and Jessie-Tibbie-Ruth behaved with such discretion, as to form a most effective tableau. Birdie, who had special leave to stay behind the curtain, pounced upon her treasure, and marched off with it to the front in time to witness the last scene.

Here Dulcie, as Cinderella, appeared in a very dirty little frock, with great black smudges on her rosy cheeks. Behind her stood her sisters with angry wondering faces, and, bending on his knee before her, Rory, the Prince's messenger, in cherry-coloured doublet, drew the small glass slipper on her dainty foot. The curtain fell amid tumults of applause, and then came calls for the chief performers—the Babes in the Wood, Sister Ann and Fatima, Dame Trot and Old King Cole—and also for Major Lennox and his nephew, who, having been working hard behind the scenes, made their bow in dress of more than picturesque disorder.

"Geoff, you dear old boy, you *have* been good!" said Judith, going up to him, and seizing hold of his arm with unusual demonstration. "Things would never have

c

gone off right without you, and you must have found it slow. The stage was simply glorious; everybody thought so."

"Lend a hand with this," said Geoff, preparing to carry off a heavy 'property;' and as they stood together in the dim light of the conservatory, he added in a very low tone of voice, "I'm not going back to Winchester any more."

"Oh, why?"

"Father and Uncle Harry have decided that I'd better go at once to the coach at Sunbury: he will have a vacancy in autumn. They say it's only waste of time to go back again to school."

"Aren't you sorry, though?" said Judy.

"Awfully! for some things," Geoff answered from the bottom of his heart. Then brightening, he added, "Only, of course, I'm glad to be getting on."

"That's always the way with boys!" said Judy thoughtfully. "They want to grow older, and get on, and be men, as quickly as they can. Now I am not a bit like that! If I could, I would stay as I am for ever. What is the use of being old? It only means worry and care and responsibility and trouble.——Yes, Aunt Dolly, did you call?"

"The little ones are in at supper," said Mrs. Lennox.

"Judy, can you keep a watch and get Birdie quietly away to bed as soon as she comes out. She is very much excited, and I dare not let her dance. Perhaps you will manage to avoid a scene."

"Oh, she will come, if I promise to put her to bed myself," said Judith. "Didn't she look a darling in Red-Riding Hood? She had such a pretty colour, and her eyes were so shy and bright. Don't keep our waltzes, Geoff: if I wait until she is asleep, I can't tell when I shall be down."

There was at least one trouble and responsibility from which Judith did not shrink.

CHAPTER III.

DOLLY'S MISSION.

" For pity melts the mind to love."
—DRYDEN.

THE summer days were long and beautiful, and when once the exciting preparations for the party were at an end, Judith and little Barbara were either driving in the pony cart, following Mrs. Lennox about the house, or playing in the garden, thus leaving the schoolroom in peaceful possession of the twins, who seized the opportunity for grand doings with their dolls, an amusement they conducted with originality and spirit. They had collected nearly fifty little china figures, varying in height from two to six or seven inches, and with these they acted the whole story of a kingdom—Babyland.

Like that of most nations, the early history of Babyland was buried in obscurity, nothing definite being known before the landing of Duke Henry, a charming little hero in black velvet, to whom not the smallest opposition appears to have been offered, and who quickly became the idol of his new people. He it was who founded the beautiful capital, called in loving memory of him Henrystown, in which Colonel Enderby himself took real interest, even presenting the corporation with many of the public buildings; and all Dolly and Dulcie's pocket-money not appropriated by Judy for the good of the living community, was spent in adding to its treasures. It was indeed a pretty little town, formed entirely of Swiss woodwork, and conveniently situated in the lower division of a sort of cupboard or bureau which hung against the schoolroom wall: the upper part belonged to Judith, and opened separately in two glass doors, but the twins' compartment shut up by a board, which, when pulled forward, made a shelf or tableland upon the outskirts of the city. The Town Hall, a large building, raised on a slight eminence, with balcony and verandah, stood at the back, and was well supplied with materials for public business; for originally it had been an inkstand, only sacrificed in a moment of tender-heartedness to compensate Dolly for the loss of a double tooth. Very cheerful were the streets of little *châlets* with their bright green window-shutters and sloping roofs held down by stones, and here and there was a more ambitious-looking farm of darker wood, with possibly a pump in the courtyard, a kennel for the dog, dishes and platters drying in the sun, and an outside staircase leading to the granary. An ivory church with double belfry stood conspicuously in one corner, and the thoroughfares were brisk and busy with mules and goats and cows on their way to pasturage or market, men with long Swiss horns attended by St. Bernard dogs carrying tiny spirit barrels round their necks, peasants from the neighbouring villages bearing on their backs great loads of common kitchen utensils and other things for sale, while in the centre of the chief street was a lovely little model, in light wood, of a hay cart from the Black Forest, drawn by two big sleepy-looking oxen, and driven by a picturesque manikin in dark brown.

But the real centre and heart of the kingdom was the enormous red brick palace, commonly called the babyhouse, and here all sorts of arts and manufactures had their rise; a grocery business, a china shop, a public library and reading-room, and a school of cookery were each tried in turn, the last suggested by the present of a most elaborate set of pots and pans, presided over by a tin man-cook, evidently of French origin. His thin and delicate appearance was a striking contrast to the sturdy Babylanders, and it was no wonder that at last he utterly gave way, and broke in two somewhere about the middle. Brave Babylanders were not particular to an arm or leg or two, but this was a calamity beyond endurance or repair, and there was nothing for it but to get an old Vesuvian match-box from their father, and give him an impressive funeral in the shrubbery. So far, so good; but the twins further thought it necessary to make a cardboard tombstone for his grave, on which in all simplicity they wrote a sacred text, and were both hurt and astonished by the indignant sermon which Judith preached to them, commenting severely on their profanity, and throwing the objectionable inscription into the fire.

At length, by the wishes of his people, the good Duke Henry assumed the title of Prince, and hereditary sovereignty was conferred upon his family; then he died, and for a time the palace was occupied by Prince Edward, whose exact relationship to him was just a little doubtful, as Dolly and Dulcie could not quite make up their minds. However, he was at any rate the lawful ruler, and even had he not been, he possessed such superhuman virtues that nothing short of madness could have left him in retirement. Resembling Duke Henry in height and appearance, although a trifle stouter and less sad, he like him wore a royal suit of velvet with the badge of monarchy—a small clasp-knife of tortoiseshell, hanging by a golden girdle round his waist. His brother Alfred had a similar costume, but was weaker in character: he was of a gentle and sensitive artist nature, and had an enormous paint-box with a picture of the Lake of Geneva on the outside. Then there were two sisters, the sweet womanly Princess Laura, who was generally exquisitely dressed, and Princess Mabel, bright and wayward, who submitted willingly to no one but the elder brother she adored: for her sake one of the state apartments in the palace was turned into a schoolroom, and Geoff and Judith painted a delightful set of maps to hang upon the walls, chiefly of the lesser isles of Scotland, although one great achievement was supposed to give the geological structure of all France. In spite of the many calls of state, young Edward managed to direct his sisters' studies, and took upon himself the entire instruction of a very little pickle of a brother, Prince Hector, who possessed the advantage of movable arms and legs, and had once been a golden charm hanging from Aunt Dolly's watch-chain.

But trouble fell on Babyland. Close to it lay that neighbouring realm of Boxland, which had always been a dangerous rival; and after many trifling acts of aggression and hostility, in Prince Edward's reign war was openly declared by George the king, once known better as the famous cricketer, George Parr. At the time of his arrival on the scene, Rory was going through the schoolboy stage of hero-worship of professional bats and bowlers, and from him the twins acquired an accurate knowledge of their photographs and a hazy notion of their several capabilities. Three of the dolls—all of them his present—were clad in flannels and bore distinguished names, and he had made them neat little bats adapted to their size. There were many fierce battles, but the contest was unequal, for Babyland had not a standing army, and although (with the exception of a dark-haired little Willie, who was constitutionally unable to quit his orange-coloured bath, and the blind boy Richard Cavendish, who with his brother Albert lodged in one of the palace chimneys) the nation to a man arose, Boxland was in the end victorious, and the royal family were driven away from their native land. King George, residing in his enemy's palace, must have bitterly regretted the jovial cricket season of his life, for there was he left in solitary grandeur, while public interest centred in the little dark green box where the exiled brothers and sisters found a refuge; with one faithful attendant in blue-and white-checked flannel, Alick Rowley, who followed their wanderings, performed the housework, carried Prince Hector when he was tired, and grew to be Prince Edward's trusted friend.

One afternoon when Dolly and Dulcie were in the full swing of their interesting game, Mrs. Lennox brought up a visitor to their schoolroom. This was Mrs. Burnell, a lady who with her husband had lately come to live at Oakleigh, a house which was about a quarter of a mile from Woodlands by the road, although the gardens lay together, divided only by a steep and grassy bank sloping from Colonel Enderby's grounds. A large square pond was in the lower property. The Burnells had one child, a boy of ten, who some months previously had met with a terrible accident at school, falling from a tree in the playground, and injuring his spine so severely that the only hope of recovery was in two or three years of perfect rest. The little Enderbys had never been near enough to speak to him, but they sometimes saw him in the distance, lying upon a couch in the garden on warm bright days. Mrs. Burnell had come to ask the twins to go next day and dine with him: as she was obliged to be away all the afternoon, and Eric would be glad of young companions.

"It is so dull for him, poor boy," she said, laying her hand gently on little Dulcie's shoulder, "and I know you will be good to him, even if in manner he should seem a little cold. Think what it must be not to be able to run about."

"It must be dreadful!" said Dolly from her heart.

"And what nice dolls you have!" continued Mrs. Burnell, picking up one off the table. "This is a pretty little fellow! what is his name?"

"Prince Edward," said incautious Dolly, blushing hotly at her own mistake, for the twins were shy about their royalty, and only by accident revealed their noble birth.

"Really! you funny children!" said Mrs. Burnell with a smile. "And are these all princes and princesses too? Will you bring Prince Edward with you to-morrow when you come? Eric will be interested to see him, I am sure."

"Dolly, how *could* you?" said Dulcie in mild reproach, as the door closed behind the elders.

"Yes, wasn't it stupid? Never mind, we can put him

in our pocket, and perhaps Mrs. Burnell may never tell about him, or Eric may forget to ask. Dulcie, I don't think I like her."

"Don't you?" said Dulcie inquiringly, having no special feeling on the point herself.

"No. Why did she call us funny children?" said Dolly, firing up. "I hate being called a funny child. And I don't see why" (with renewed indignation) "it should be any funnier to play with a prince than with a butcher's boy or chimney sweep."

But Mrs. Burnell did *not* forget to mention Prince Edward; and that very evening a note from her arrived for Dolly, in which she said that Eric would be glad if the little girls would bring, not only him, but all the boy-dolls they possessed. They were a curious assemblage —Mr. Richardson, the grocer, in a suit of rusty black; his two sons, Jim and Charlie; King George in a gorgeous crimson cloak; the exiled princes; Alick Rowley and a brother cricketer; a German prince, Lionel Leopold by name; Albert and Richard Cavendish; little Willie in his bath; Ferdinand Fordati, a very stout Greek boy in velvet coat and scarlet knickerbockers; a prim-looking courtier called Sir Thomas Eden; and many others. The children put them all carefully in a little basket with their indoor shoes, and started rather gravely on their expedition. They were to come home by themselves at five o'clock.

Mrs. Burnell, in her bonnet, met them in the hall; and when they had taken off their hats, she led them at once to a little room where her son was lying. Imagination had pictured him a gentle, placid invalid, with fair hair clustering round his forehead, like the good little choristers they read of in their story-books: instead, they saw a bright, intelligent face, with large and very dark brown eyes full of mischief, and a sensitive mouth, spoiled by its look of restless discontent. His very pale complexion contrasted sharply with his short black hair. Dinner was waiting on a table beside him, and the little girls sat down, feeling very shy and silent under Eric's critical survey. Mrs. Burnell hovered about for a few minutes, hoping to set them at their ease; but her carriage was announced, and with kind words to the visitors she went away.

Eric instantly began to talk. "What is the name of your brother?" he asked. "Not the big one—a fellow with curly hair, I mean."

"Rory," answered Dolly; and Dulcie kindly gave him the whole catalogue of names—"Geoffrey, Judith-Mary, Roderick, Dorothea, Dulcibella, Barbara, and then there was Alan," she said.

"We are seven!" quoted Eric with a smile, "but about Rory! Has he been fishing lately *in our pond?*"

The little girls blushed crimson. Among Rory's naughtiest exploits were secret twilight expeditions with his rod to the pond which lay so near to Woodlands, and even Geoff and Judy were not allowed to know. He carefully watched his opportunities, and all fish thus obtained were cooked privately for him by the woman at the lodge, with whom he was a favourite, and formed the chief dainty at little suppers in the hayloft, to which only the twins and the children of the gardener and coachman were admitted. Dolly and Dulcie went with uneasy consciences, but Rory, who felt rather guilty and was naturally hot-tempered, grew very angry at their least remonstrance, and insisted on their presence at his feasts. Not one of them had the slightest idea that his clandestine sport had been discovered, and the sisters looked at each other in blank dismay.

"How do you know? who told you?" they exclaimed together. "Does Mr. Burnell"——

"Not quite, or Rory would have heard of it again," laughed Eric, immensely pleased with the sensation he created. "Don't be afraid," he said composedly, "I am a boy myself, and of course I wouldn't let on about him. I will tell you how it was: I was lying by the window in the other room one evening as it was getting dusk, when I saw a figure by the pond; and just as I was going to sing out to my father, who was sitting reading there, I caught sight of something that looked like a rod, and guessed pretty well what he was after. So then I kept them all away from me until it was too dark to see out there at all."

"And have you never said a word to any one?" asked Dulcie, gazing at him with unspeakable gratitude.

"Rather not! Why, my father would be awfully mad, and take the high moral tone about poaching and stealing and all that sort of thing, you know. One couldn't spoil sport, of course; so after that I had the blind drawn down an hour earlier each night, that the others mightn't see him, but if they left me alone a bit I used to lift up a corner, and peep behind it, and wish I was out there with him. Sometimes I could see him drawing in his line."

"How jolly of you not to tell!" said Dolly tenderly. "What is the matter, Dulcie? No one knows but us, and Eric won't ever say a word."

"It isn't that," said Dulcie, "but I wish," looking at Eric, "that he hadn't said that his father would call it stealing. It makes it seem such a horrid thing for one of us to do—not a bit plucky or manly, as Rory thought. Perhaps now he will promise not to go again."

"Not likely, I should think," said Eric loftily.

After dinner a maid brought Eric's cap and coat, and he was carried down upon his couch into the sunny garden, the little girls following with their basket and his book—"The Crofton Boys." There he lay for a few minutes, his white face flushed with the fatigue and pain of transit, and his lips tightly pressed together; but in a little while he roused himself and explained why he had asked to have the dolls. He was interested in the story of school life which he was reading, and thought that to act it with variations would make a capital game: he himself would be the master Mr. Tooke, and the twins could choose two other characters. A small shrub growing near his couch was the tall tree in the playground where Firth used to sit on holidays; Ferdinand Fordati should be Lamb, Mr. Richardson the usher, Prince Alfred and Prince Hector stand for Dale and little Harry, and Prince Edward for Hugh Proctor, the hero of the tale. But here an unexpected difficulty arose. The children had grown very friendly over the knowledge of their common secret, but Dolly and Dulcie's loyal feelings rebelled aginst the illustrious exiles being treated as ordinary boys, and they care-

"DOLLY WAS ABOUT TO ANSWER SHARPLY WHEN SHE WAS STOPPED BY DULCIE'S PLEADING FACE"

Chap. III.

fully explained their exalted rank: he might do what he liked with the rest, said Dolly firmly, but these should be put aside; they were princes, and must be treated with due respect. Eric listened with amusement, but after a time grew angry. He was accustomed to his own way in little things, and openly declared (what indeed was evident) that he had no patience with such nonsense. He didn't consider they were dolls at all—only girls played with dolls—they were puppets to act with, like the marionettes he had once seen at a theatre.

Dolly was about to answer sharply, when she was stopped by Dulcie's pleading face; and remembering from how many pleasures Eric was debarred, the little girls in the end gave way. The game was very spirited. Eric's memory or imagination supplied such queer speeches and adventures for the boys, that Dulcie quite forgot her prince's wrongs; and although his degradation rankled fitfully in Dolly's mind, she was also carried away by intense enjoyment, until there came an insult to which she could not possibly submit. According to Eric, the game required that Prince Edward, as Hugh Proctor, should be handed over to the usher to be flogged. Dolly in his name objected, but as she was only personating Hugh's elder brother Philip,

Mr. Tooke calmly rebuked her for impertinent interference and ordered an imposition of fifty lines: she answered hotly, and disregarding her sister's bright suggestion that Albert Cavendish as Holt should generously propose to bear the punishment instead, a war of words began, resulting in Dolly snatching up her treasure, and rushing off in guilty triumph down the avenue as fast as her little legs could go.

"What a jolly rage she's in!" said Eric, turning wearily upon his pillow. "Well, I suppose it comes of trying to play with *girls*."

"Shall I ask Rory to come and see you some day?" said Dulcie, looking at him with wistful eyes.

Perhaps this dear child had hitherto had no harder trial than to stay patiently with Eric while her whole heart was longing to console her twin, and the thought that Dolly might reproach her for not following was almost more than she could bear; and Dolly would be sorry soon, and she would not be there to comfort her. Eric, with his curious knack of understanding people, was perfectly aware of Dulcie's struggle, but he was tired and dissatisfied with his own conduct, and would not make the necessary effort to be kind. He lay back languidly and took so little interest in the game that she was thankful for a rather cross suggestion, that if she liked she might fetch another book and read aloud: and her sweet little voice went on steadily until the clock in the Woodlands tower chimed the hour of five; then at the end of the next paragraph she paused.

"Time's up!" said Eric mockingly. "You can go now. Aren't you glad?"

"I should like to come again and see you," said the child evasively, lingering for a kinder word; but Eric only answered gruffly, "Please yourself. Good-bye," and coldly touched her outstretched hand.

Dolly met her at the Woodlands gate. Not caring to account for her speedy reappearance, she had hung about in an aimless manner since her return, waiting for her sister, and finding the afternoon very long and tedious. She had crouched among the bushes when the boys went past, and altogether seemed rather crestfallen, but neither she nor Dulcie made any special reference to the quarrel, and at tea they gave composed and quiet answers to the few questions asked. Mrs. Lennox had a general impression that they had not enjoyed their day, but their small experiences were thrown completely into the shade by the news the boys had brought—that their tutor Mr. Martindale, the curate of Norrington, had accepted the offer of a living in

Devonshire, and was going there next month. A friend, Mr. Lincoln, was coming in his place.

The twins remained in the schoolroom when the rest had gone—Dolly, who at tea had scarcely eaten or spoken, standing by a little table in the window, looking out. She did not turn her head, when Dulcie came and stood beside her, but gave a sort of groan, "I wish I hadn't been so horrid."

"Yes," said Dulcie gently; then after a little pause "You will have to tell him so?"

Silence reigned for a few moments. "I hate *saying* I'm sorry," said Dolly, with a shake.

"But why," said Dulcie, "if you are?"

The Enderbys were by no means little saints of children. They had their private squabbles and disagreements, which without the pretence of excessive penitence or magnanimity on either side, they forgave and forgot from the depths of their generous warm-hearted natures; but there was among them a great contempt for anything that was cowardly or mean, and by no milder names could Dolly term desertion of a boy who could not follow her. It was not a fair fight, for she had taken advantage of his infirmity, and Dolly had never felt so ashamed and sorry in her life.

An hour later the same evening Eric was lying by

himself upstairs. His parents had gone down to dinner, but he had said he was too tired to be moved and would rather be alone. He was bitterly disappointed. Often and often had he lain and listened for the merry voices of the children, and watched them coming into sight, and though Geoff and Judith were too old and Barbara too young to inspire much interest, for the friendship of Rory and the twins he longed with his whole heart. It was all very well to whistle to himself the "Miller of the Dee," but the defiant burden

> "I care for nobody, no, not I!
> And nobody cares for me!"

could not banish the thought of Dulcie's gentleness and Dolly's bright indignant face. She was decidedly his favourite, and he liked her all the better for her loyalty. Looking listlessly through the window (for it was too early yet for Rory), he saw two tiny figures scrambling with difficulty down the bank dividing the two gardens, and with a strange throb of delight he recognised the flowing hair and pink print dresses of the twins. Perhaps they were coming to keep a look-out for their brother, and Eric began to ponder how a system of secret signalling could be devised: his lamp in a fixed position would show when the coast was clear.—But at the foot of the bank, the children caught hold of each other's hands, and ran along the edge of the pond and up the lawn, until under the shadow of the house they were lost to sight: then he was sure he heard his mother's voice speaking to them in the hall, followed by a gentle footstep, and in another minute Dolly, with rosy cheeks and kindling eyes, stood upon the threshold.

"O Eric! I am so sorry I was cross!"

Eric tried to speak, but something seemed to choke him. He held out his thin hand and smiled, and Dolly came up fearlessly. "It was such a shame," she said, "when you were so awfully jolly about Rory too! Even Dulcie thought it horrid, and the boys would scarcely speak to me if they knew what I had done. I will do anything to make it up," she said with touching earnestness, "only *please* don't touch Prince Edward, for it hurts us so. You are a boy, and so of course you cannot understand," she added with a touch of womanly disdain, "but Babyland seems real unless we are reminded, and Rory is always good to him, and gives him pennies when he can; for they are exiles now, and oh! so very poor!"

"Is Rory coming to fish to-night?" asked Eric shyly, glad to change the subject, but Dolly shook her head. "Won't you forgive me, Eric?" she said wistfully.

"Mrs. Burnell said I might come up, but I wasn't to stay long, and besides we shall be missed at home; no one knows that we are here. We slid down the bank on purpose, and got our frocks in such a mess: Elizabeth will wonder what we have been doing."

"I hope you won't get into a scrape about it," said Eric, holding her by her slender arm. "Of course I forgive you, Dolly; only you see I was just as bad as you were, and so you will have to forgive me too. What queer things girls are!" he went on slowly. "Do you know, I rather wish you were my sister?"

"Do you?" said Dolly, blushing. "And may I come again and play?"

"Oh yes!" the boy said eagerly; "and can't you come alone sometimes?"

"Not without Dulcie, do you mean?" said Dolly, wondering. "I never go anywhere without Dulcie. She is waiting for me down below."

"I will make it all right with her," said Eric the wilful. "You see you are more of a man than she is, and I am not used to having a lot of girls about. Good-night, if you are really going. Dolly, you may kiss me, if you like."

And thus began for Eric Burnell a new interest, which brightened all his life; the mutual fancy between him and Dolly soon ripening into a confiding friendship, to which even Dulcie's presence was a slight restraint; and although their love for one another was not the least bit lessened, the little sisters found, as time went on, that their different occupations sometimes kept them separate for hours. Dolly's visits to her friend were very frequent, for a flight of wooden steps, laid down the bank at his suggestion, made communication easy, and even when the holidays were over, nearly every day she found her way to him at twelve or five o'clock. It was her great delight to make him happy, and under her bright influence his temper certainly improved. He was an active daring boy, spirited and manly beyond his years, when the accident occurred, which at first he bore so bravely. Bit by bit he related to Dolly the story of that time, and how, with all his might, he strove for courage to hide how much he suffered, and not let one murmur or complaint pass his lips. In a few short weeks, he thought—long though they seemed to him—he should go back to school and take his place among the boys as a sort of little hero. He used to count the days and hours to the beginning of next half, and there was nothing he liked better than the full accounts of cricket and athletic sports which kind companions sent to cheer him. But as that longed-for date drew near, and he asked how soon he should be well again, no one answered him. Parents, nurse, and doctor tried to change the subject, until, with misery unspeakable, he found out for himself the truth they had not dared to tell—that week by week there had been no real improvement, and that each sound or movement jarred the injured nerves as much as ever. It was only when he struggled with a terror lest this helplessness might be for life, that it was broken to him gently that he must be an invalid for years.

Little Dolly, listening to the storm of troubled words in which Eric told his story, could only stroke his hand or gaze with pitying eyes into his face; but he liked her touch and sympathy, and although she could not understand the fulness of his sorrow, he had never spoken with such total unreserve. He told how from the moment when he knew his fate he lost heart entirely. Where was the use of trying to be brave, of clinging to old memories, of keeping up an interest in the friends whose equal he would never be again, whose work and play he hourly pined to join, while lying helpless like a log, and knowing that by the time his strength returned they would have in both so far outstripped him as to leave them scarcely anything in common? He did not care to write to them or see them, and now, no doubt, he would add bitterly, they had forgotten him. Yes, it was his own fault if they had! He knew he had been cross, and rude, and ungracious; and that if he had let them, they would have come sometimes and pitied him, and then have gone away and told each other that little Burnell was so awfully changed and altered, and had no fun or spirit left. He couldn't stand that, of course; and though he was often dull and lonely, he didn't want any one to stay with him *out of kindness*, and Dolly had better go, too, if she were tired of listening to his talk.

"O Eric! when I love you so?" said Dolly in reproach.

It was no wonder that lying there, day after day, his life grew weary and monotonous, and that he felt the want of something fresh to do. His father and mother were very kind, and pitied him extremely, but they were practical busy people, not naturally fond of children, who looked upon his restless discontent as a feature of his illness, instead of trying to find out new subjects to divert his thoughts. Dolly, feeling unable to meet the difficulty, after the fashion of her family carried it to Judy, who was found dangerously climbing up the steep and slanting roof of the conservatory, Rory, in his parting moments, having dared her to perform the feat. When at last she reached the ground in safety and high spirits, she was ready to give full attention to Dolly's question, and the sisters repaired to the tool-house to think the matter over. Judith perched herself dexterously upon the grindstone, and Dolly turned a 'wisket' upside down.

"He hates reading, and netting, and puzzles," she explained thoughtfully; "he has so much of them; and he says that natural history is all humbug when he can't find anything himself. You know he can't climb trees for eggs, or catch butterflies, or go anywhere to pick up stones or shells; and though he would like to understand about chemistry, his father won't let him try experiments, and without them, he says, the books are slow and have such dreadfully hard words. He is tired of draughts, and patience, and beggar-my-neighbour," continued Dolly, adding from the depths of her experience, "and then a boy can't really care for dolls and wool-work, even if he doesn't call them 'rot.' Unless you can help us, there seems nothing left." She gazed imploringly at Judith as she spoke.

Miss Judy shook her elf-locks and made an unsuccessful try for her favourite attitude—sitting with one leg tucked beneath her—but this the nature of the grindstone would not permit: then with a triumphant little whistle, she suddenly exclaimed—

"I know! I have it! Doll, don't you remember that splendid book, 'Frank Fairleigh,' that Geoff went wild about last holidays? Rory and I thought him awfully silly, until he made us read it too, and we were just as bad. I laughed so much one night that I upset a cup of coffee all over my blue dress, and Elizabeth was frantically cross. Some day I'll tell you some of the stories as you are not old enough to read them yet, but I was going to say that Uncle Harry told us it was written by a cripple who had to lie upon a sofa all day long, just as Eric does. We could hardly believe him. It is so full of life and go, you know,—what Uncle Harry calls rollicking,—and one always imagines invalids are rather serious, at least I know I do. Well, don't you think Eric could do something of the kind? He can have a lot of my old copybooks and write between the lines, and you could help him, and perhaps *I'll* do a piece every now and then. I've often thought that I should like to write a book," said candid Judith, "only it would take such hours and hours, so that I shouldn't at all mind getting you on a bit sometimes, and in fact, should rather like it. Come on! we shall be late for dinner."

Eric, fortunately, was charmed with this idea of authorship, which gave him plenty to think about when Dolly was away; and their tale made rapid progress.

Dulcie was the critic, and used to be hurried in great triumph to Eric's sofa when a peculiarly thrilling passage was achieved; and she gave them such encouragement, that emboldened by it, they looked forward with an awful and delicious sort of terror to showing their work at Christmas-time to Rory. He had had a letter on the subject.

"My Dear Rory,—If any of you do anything *very* naughty, please will you let us know, that Eric may put it in his book. Your affectionate sister,

"Dorothea Enderby."

CHAPTER IV.

A BIRD OF PASSAGE.

"O light wise swallow! has none of your band
  Caught ever a glimpse of that wonderful land,
    Where love is so true,
    It lasteth life through,
  And never seeks change, yet always is new!

"We have travelled far to the East and West—
  In a thousand lands we have built the nest,
    But the tender skies,
    Where love never dies,
  Must be sought not here, but in Paradise."
                    —*The Wisdom of the Swallow.*

BUT if Dolly had found a mission, Dulcie had found a friend, and this was the new curate, Mr. Lincoln, who, though quiet and reserved in general society, quickly became a favourite in the village, and startled every one by the power and force of his Sunday sermons. Mr. Leigh, his rector, was an invalid, and away in Italy. It was not the life Hugh Lincoln would have chosen a few years ago, when everything appeared to smile upon the scheme which he had cherished from his boyhood, that of becoming a missionary and carrying the light of gospel truth to other lands; but as time went on, difficulty after difficulty arose, and after a dark season of rebellion, he had learnt at last to tarry the Lord's leisure, and to try and be contented with the path marked out for him.

It was in the cottages that he and Dulcie met. A little group of houses stood almost opposite the Woodlands gate, and when Dolly became absorbed in Eric Burnell, and Dulcie's time hung heavily on hand, her nurse Elizabeth arranged that she should sometimes read to three or four old women who lived there. Hugh Lincoln came one day when she was seated in a high arm-chair, with the big Bible resting on a small deal table, and the old dame in the chimney corner listening eagerly to the well-beloved words. It was a pretty little picture, and as he paused a moment on the threshold to observe it, his great Scotch collie dog took advantage of the open door, and rushed with good-natured violence upon the child.

"Lassie! Lassie! come off, Lassie!" called the curate

anxiously, fearing that she would be frightened; but Dulcie's arms were round her neck, and she was gazing in an ecstasy of admiration into the beseeching eyes.

"I never saw anything so beautiful!" she murmured softly to herself.

"You are sure you are not frightened," said Mr. Lincoln; and then Dulcie raised her head, and answered with reproachful emphasis—

"We are *never* afraid of dogs, unless we *know* they bite;" while the old woman added with a chuckle—

"I would like to see what would scare *any* o' them childer!"

One autumn afternoon, Dulcie bowled her hoop down to the front gate, to watch for her father returning from his ride. It was Saturday, and Dolly was with Eric, the boys away, and Judith in the house with Birdie, who had grown more delicate than ever, and in this damp and chilly weather was seldom allowed to leave the nurseries. As she stood there, looking at a little chaffinch perched upon a bush outside, a big boy, with a basket of provisions from the village shop, came whistling up the road, and carelessly picking up a stone, shied it at the bird which, to his astonishment, he hit. Instantly, Dulcie, with crimson cheeks, was tugging

"I NEVER THOUGHT I SHOULD HIT IT, MISS"
Chap. IV.

A Bird of Passage.

at the gate, and bounding across the road, she turned indignantly upon the lad.

"You naughty, wicked boy! how dare you, how could you do it?" she said passionately; then stroking the little ball of feathers which she had lifted from the ground, her tears began to fall. "O birdie, birdie! what can I do for you?" she said.

Stunned or frightened, it lay in her tiny palm as still as death.

"I never thought as I should hit it, miss," the boy said, drawing near, "and maybe 'tisn't dead at all."

Dulcie's fingers closed over it at once. "Oh, go away, *please* go away," she said.

Mr. Lincoln came upon them suddenly, as he turned a corner of the road, the little damsel nursing her treasure tenderly, and the boy beside her, awkward and shamefaced. At the sight of the parson he moved away, and Dulcie looked up piteously in answer to a voice—

"Well, little one, is anything the matter?"

Children and animals always found their way directly to Mr. Lincoln's heart. In another minute he was studying the case with the deepest interest. With his finger he felt that the heart of the small sufferer had not ceased to beat, and although its leg was broken, he had sufficient skill in surgery to put it into splints. Dulcie ran into the house for leave to go with him to his lodgings and see the operation, and he promised her a cage which had belonged to a canary of his that was dead. They walked together down the High Street, he talking all the while, and telling her how to treat her captive until it was cured.

"It will pine and fret at first, most likely; you cannot make it happy in a moment, but if you are kind to it and feed it as I tell you every day, gradually it will come to know and care for you, and, perhaps, when the cage doors are opened and you set it free, it will not care to leave you all at once. Perhaps it will come back willingly to its prison; people have done that too, you know, in thought, and surely that ought to make one more contented in captivity, and not try to beat one's wings against the iron bars."

Dulcie looked puzzled, and the curate pressed the little hand he held.

"You think you do not understand?"

"Perhaps Judy might," said Dulcie humbly.

"The tall girl with red hair?" said Mr. Lincoln, smiling. "Do you know, Dulcie, I believe that dogs and children understand a great deal more than people think? When I am tired out and lonely, why does

Lassie get up from her comfortable rug and thrust her head upon my knee? And if I speak impatiently, she does not go away, but waits with fond persistence until I am myself again. And children do what is much the same thing. Haven't you ever gathered a rose from your garden, Mite, or picked a dozen of the finest strawberries, to give to some one whom you have heard sighing or seen winking away a furtive tear? You don't believe that strawberries and roses are a cure for heartaches, do you? any more than Lassie thinks that to have her paw to hold is the height of human bliss; but it is all part of a wonderful unspoken language of love and sympathy—which we often do not prize enough until it is too late. Well, here we are!" he added suddenly, stopping in front of a small house.

"I knew that this was where you lived," said Dulcie confidentially.

They went into a good-sized sitting-room, plainly furnished, but with plenty of books and pictures and little possessions to make it homelike, and Lassie came to greet them at the door. Then, at a word of command, she lay down on the rug, while Mr. Lincoln fetched the things which he required. Dulcie knelt on a high chair with her elbows on the table, watching the skilful way in which he set the broken limb, and when once she hid her face, shrinking lest the bird should give some evidence of pain, she was bidden to hold something that he wanted, and told gently that brave women must never shirk the sight of suffering they can comfort or relieve.

"Isn't it a good thing this did not happen later in the season?" he said to her, "for your bird is a bird of passage, and when November comes, it and its comrades will fly away from our dull skies to warm and sunny lands. It would be hard, wouldn't it, to be left behind?"

"Yes," said Dulcie, "but haven't I seen a chaffinch in the winter? I thought they came at the same time as the robins to be fed."

"Ah, the hen-birds stay in England. Now, this box with cotton-wool will make a sort of bed for your invalid to lie on, and here is a small packet of birdseed for you to take. Where do you think that you will hang your cage?"

"I expect we shall give it to Birdie, my little sister," explained Dulcie. "She is delicate, you know, and can't go out much now."

"I shall come in a few days to look after my patient," said Mr. Lincoln, "and now I must take you home. Come, Lassie, you shall go with us!"

Dolly and Judith were in the schoolroom, the latter sprawling on the rug and frowning over some Latin, which, because it was taught her by her father, was her favourite study. The twins retired as usual to the window, discussing the afternoon's events, and at once deciding that they would give the bird to Barbara.

"Won't she be pleased?" said Dolly, "but we can't take it to her just yet, for Dr. Grey is in the nursery with father."

"How often he comes now, nearly every day," said Dulcie. "Birdie must be very ill, worse than Eric even, for he only goes to Oakleigh twice a week."

"Shut up, children," called out Judy crossly. "How can any one learn anything while you are making such a row?"

Poor Judith! it was anxiety that lent such sharpness to her tone. The twins were putting into words the nameless dread against which she was struggling, and she could not bear to listen to their idle talk. She would not ask a question of her father or Elizabeth, and avoided being alone with them, but every moment that was possible she spent with the beloved little sister, who now never left the house, and seemed to grow smaller and paler every day. The chaffinch's cage was hung up in the nursery in full view of the little sofa where the other Birdie lay for many hours, and she watched its progress with intense delight, but her own recovery was less steady; and the chaffinch was hopping about merrily on one leg and pecking vigorously at its food, while, day by day, wee Barbara's strength was failing, and her brown eyes glowing with a deeper light.

Colonel Enderby and Judith were in the nursery with Birdie one November evening while Elizabeth was down at supper, and it was the favourite hour in the whole day to the little invalid, who, though often languid and sleepy in the morning, generally revived towards afternoon. She was always patient and cheerful, and welcomed her visitors with smiles. The little couch was drawn close to the fire, which blazed brightly, and Jessie-Tibbie-Ruth dosed comfortably on the rug, every now and then blinking her green eyes sleepily. The ninepin boys were propped against the back of the sofa, looking at a great scrapbook which was lying on their mother's lap, its weight supported by their kind Aunt Judy who, kneeling on the floor, explained the pictures with an occasional appeal to her father, sitting opposite in a big arm-chair.

"Poor little boys!" said Birdie, touching the round heads tenderly. "They have had the scarlatina, and are very weak. That is why they go out so seldom now."

Colonel Enderby also had a book upon his knee, but he was not reading. Very sad was the expression of his face, and he stole frequent glances towards his little daughters—Judith, full of health and energy, and Barbara's fragile little form, nestling lovingly against her.

"Don't you think, Miss Judy," said the sweet little voice, "that if to-morrow is warm and bright, we might let my chaffinch go?"

"Yes, perhaps," said Judy doubtfully. "It seems all right again; but shan't you miss it very much?"

"Oh yes!" and the child's lip quivered for a moment, but she went on with a smile, "only it will be so happy, and Mr. Lincoln said to Dulcie that when November came we must be sure and let it go: it would want so much to fly away."

"I suppose it must be dreadful for birds like these—birds of passage, aren't they?—to be shut up in a cage when winter comes," said Judith thoughtfully. "Fancy a swallow near a window where it sees a cold grey world and naked trees, and soppy grass with bits of stick and withered leaves scattered all about, and knowing all the time that its companions and relations have flown away to sunshine, and blue skies, and orange-trees, and mangoes perhaps. (I don't quite know where swallows go.) How desolate and lonely it must feel, and how it must long to kill itself against the bars!"

"Do the birds fly *here?*" asked Birdie, looking at some sketches of the Hoogley river in their father's Indian scrapbook, which was only lent to the two girls as an especial treat. "Don't you wish that we were swallows, so that we might see it too? O Judy! can't we ask him now?"

Judith nodded, and looked up with kindling eyes.

"Father, we have a favour to ask you," she began. "Will you promise to take us both to India some day, when I am grown up, and the twins and Rory are at school, and when Birdie is not old enough to go there with them? It would be so glorious, you and I and she, and perhaps Geoffrey will be out already with his corps. Don't say No, at any rate!"

"Oh, darling father, please say Yes," said Barbara.

"It is not a sudden thought, either, father," continued Judy earnestly. "You say I never do consider things, but we have often talked this over, haven't we, Birdie? and we both wish it more than anything. Or, wouldn't it do for me *instead* of school? People say that foreign travel opens the mind; and we might go when Birdie is well again, and perhaps the voyage would make her strong?"

"Will you promise, father?" said the child.

"When Birdie is well again." It was anguish to the father to sit and listen to those words, knowing that that time would never come; and Judy's eyes fell quickly beneath the unutterable sadness of his look. A knock at the door spared him a reply; Elizabeth had come to take Miss Barbara to bed, but she begged so earnestly to stay a little longer, that she was allowed to say her evening hymn with Judith before she went away. The sisters said alternate verses, and Birdie, with folded hands, knelt reverently upon her sofa, while Judith stood upright beside her, her head a little turned, so that her father could not see her face. Why did her voice sound husky when she had to say—

> "Every spring the sweet young flowers
>   Open bright and gay,
> Till the chilly autumn hours
>   Wither them away.
> There's a land we have not seen
> Where the trees are always green"?

Then Barbara's clear, sweet treble took up the story—

> "Little birds sing songs of praise
>   All the summer long,
> But in colder, shorter days,
>   They forget their song.
> There's a place where angels sing
> Ceaseless praises to their King."

And to her turn came also the triumphant promise of the last verse—

> " Who shall go to that bright land ?
>   All who do the right ;
> Holy children there shall stand
>   In their robes of white,
> For that Heaven, so bright and blest,
> Is our everlasting rest."

"Judy," said Colonel Enderby after a little pause, "when you have taken Birdie to bed, come back here to me. Good night, my darling. God bless and keep my little Barbara."

And then he walked to the window, and pushing aside the curtain, looked out into the night.

You know what he had to tell her, but Judith never forgot the tenderness with which he confirmed the dread foreboding which for weeks had haunted her, and told her that their little Birdie's days on earth were numbered, and they must teach her to look forward to her heavenly home. Hers had been no ordinary delicacy ; he and her mother and Elizabeth had known how small was the hope that she would grow to womanhood. She was a "bird of passage" on her way to brighter and more sunny regions, and they must try and be thankful for the summer-time of her brief sojourn here.

Miss Judy did not cry. In bed that night her tears flowed freely, and her courage broke down utterly in solitude; but just then she was not only stunned and bewildered, but something in her father's manner seemed to awe her into calm. It was as if a guardian-angel were coming for the little sister whose life had been so innocent and loving, and Judith knew that Birdie would be ready to obey the call. When her father told her the next morning that she would not recover, it was no shock to her, and she learnt easily to dwell upon the image of a Saviour who called little children unto Him. Very soon the household grew accustomed to her bright and confident allusions to seeing "mother and Alan again in heaven," and, as through November she grew paler and weaker, patience and gentleness never seemed to fail her. There was no sadness in her presence. She cried a little when her chaffinch flew away, but people were very kind and sent her flowers and toys, and she was almost always happy. Judith scarcely ever left her in those last few weeks, and the child grew restless and uneasy if she were absent for an hour. Colonel Enderby insisted that a certain time each day should be spent in out-door exercise, and that half her nights should be undisturbed, but beyond this he never interfered, and he settled with Miss Gresley that for the present her eldest pupil should be released from lessons. And with unselfish courage was Miss Judy's work performed. It was chiefly her brave, cheerful words which kindled in Birdie's soul the vivid faith in God and Heaven which robbed the passage thitherward of all terror, it was in her arms the little one was oftenest soothed to rest, and, what was by far the hardest task when her heart seemed nearly breaking with the agony of parting, she had strength to put aside her sorrow, and be the brightest and most cheery playmate of them all.

Pepper, the puppy, and Jessie-Tibbie-Ruth slept placidly for hours on the bed from which their little mistress was to rise no more, and the beloved ninepins were constantly beside her.

"Miss Judy, when people die and ask other people to take care of their children, what are the other people called?"

"I don't quite understand," said Judith. "Do you mean guardians, dear?"

"No, it wasn't that," said Birdie. "Rory read it in a book; it was a longer word, I think."

"Trustees?—protectors?—what can it be?" said Judy. "You surely don't mean executors?"

"'Secutor, that is it," repeated Birdie complacently. "Miss Judy, you will be *my* 'secutor, and take care of all my boys?"

"Of course I will, my darling."

"Poor little boys, they will miss me very much," said Barbara gravely, "but you will be good to them and talk to them about me, and oh, Judy, shall you bring them to put flowers upon my grave, as we used to do for mother and Alan?"

"I shall come myself," said poor Judith, steadying her voice with difficulty. "But they are not really your children, you know."

"You shouldn't have reminded me of that," said Birdie pathetically, "when I am always trying to forget it. And oh! promise, promise" (she sat up and looked excited) "that you will never undress them and mix them up, or let people call them—*ninepins.*"

"Never, never," said Judith.

"And don't shut them up *too* much in a drawer," said Birdie, moved by the remembrance of her own misdeeds. "Perhaps I haven't been very kind to Laura—will you put her on the bed, please, for a little, now? but my story-books say that there is always something that people are sorry for when they die, and I daresay Dulcie will make it up to her in time. Dulcie always liked her; I might have given her to Dulcie long ago."

"Aren't you talking too much, my darling? You will be so tired. Everything you care for shall be loved and cherished for your sake."

Contrary to expectation, the child lingered until Christmas. Geoff and Rory were called home a little earlier to see her, Uncle Harry and Aunt Dolly arrived from Ireland; but when at last the summons came, there was no one in the room with her but Judith and her father. It was at seven o'clock one evening. She had been very weary all that day, and at last her sister lay down on the bed to try to hush her in her arms to sleep. As she felt the welcome touch, Birdie moved and fondly murmured the pet name, "Miss Judy," which since her illness she had saucily adopted, and the curly head drooped heavily on Judith's shoulder. Then the sisters lay quite still; but when, half an hour later, their father rose up softly and came to look at them, he saw that, overcome with watching, only Judith was asleep; for, without a struggle, the soul of little Barbara had taken flight, and, as they prayed for her in baptism, "steadfast in faith, joyful through hope, and rooted in charity," had passed lightly through the waves of this troublesome world unto the land of everlasting life.

CHAPTER V.

DIFFICULTIES.

"Out of debt, out of danger."—Proverb.

IT was a very sad New Year that dawned for Judith, and, as her brothers and sisters grew more cheerful, her depression, on the other hand, increased. Everything had lost its interest; she wandered aimlessly about the house and garden, and was half-disposed to quarrel with the others who, much as they had loved their little sister, were beginning to resume with spirit their usual games and occupations. The laughter of the boys playing football with the gardeners sounded heartless in her ears, and, as even in Barbara's lifetime she had been jealous of the twins' absorbing love for Eric Burnell, she now perversely chose to misinterpret it as a proof that Birdie was forgotten. She was often very lonely. After two or three repulses, her brothers ceased to try and tempt her to come out and join their games, and the little girls had an uncomfortable impression that she thought them very childish. Once Dulcie, finding her in the twilight kneeling sadly by the school-room fire, ran up to her impulsively, put her arms round her and kissed her, but Judy answered hastily and in a stifled voice—

"Don't, child! you choke me. Let me go."

And Dulcie stole away again, thinking that she had displeased her, while Judith's tears fell fast, because the gesture was so like that loving little sister who was gone. Oh! for the tiny, clasping arms that she would never feel again, the rosy lips which had given their last kiss, the little voice which was to call "Miss Judy" never more. Geoff and Rory and the twins never seemed to want her now, she used to think, forgetting how she had repulsed them, and it was her only consolation that her father liked her to be constantly with him. Their companionship in Birdie's room, and mutual grief, had drawn them very close together, and Judith looked forward to a time when he would treat her as an equal, consult her and depend on her for everything, and teach her how to fill her mother's place.

Colonel Enderby was busy at this time preparing

for press the manuscript of an important work on military tactics which had taken him some years to write, and having once carelessly remarked to Judith that if she wrote a better hand she might be useful to him in copying, she spared no pains to qualify herself for the desired post. Taking possession secretly of an old volume upon engineering, she spent long hours in writing out the contents, to improve her hand and acquire the spelling of technical terms, until at last there came a day when she presented herself in her father's study with a glow on her brown cheek, and a great pile of copy-books in her arms. She knelt down by the table and began to turn them over rapidly; the earlier pages displayed a large sprawling hand adorned with enormous capitals and many blots, but gradually the writing grew more clear and neat and careful, and the last few leaves were really creditable for her age.

"Your writing, child? how much you have improved! Is it a three-volume novel of your own composing? Why, what is this?" he added, looking more closely at it. "What possessed you to make extracts from that obsolete old book?"

"Isn't it good practice?" said Miss Judy. "Do you remember once you told me, father, that if I didn't write

F

so badly, and weren't so — so incorrigibly careless, I might be a help to you in copying? Am I good enough now? I chose this book on purpose, because I thought that if I understood the technical words, I shouldn't be so likely to make mistakes."

"How long have you been doing this?" he asked.

"Not very long, only since Christmas," said Judy with pardonable pride. "I can go the pace pretty fairly now."

"And you want to be my private secretary?" said the Colonel, putting his arm affectionately round her. "Well, I shall be glad to have your help, if it is really to be relied on. Are you sure you wish it? It will take a good deal of your time."

"I know," said Judith. "I am not a bit afraid."

And in some ways this hard work and regular occupation yielded her the greatest comfort she could have had that spring. Not only was copying entrusted to her, but by degrees the care of all the literary notes and papers in the study became her charge, and her good memory and clear head were useful in finding references. She sat a great deal with her father, who, becoming more and more accustomed to her presence, himself undertook a portion of her education, gradually freeing her from schoolroom teaching; and he was rewarded by her rapid progress. Her dread of going to school intensified as the time drew nearer, and amounted to positive aversion, but she hardly ever spoke of it. There remained for her only another year of freedom, unless, indeed, before that year was over, she became so necessary to her father that he could not bring himself to part with her; and this vague hope grew stronger day by day. It was in her nature to devote herself to some one, and she studied to render him every little service that was in her power. She was growing very fast and looked thin and delicate, but disliked the least allusion to her health.

Easter was very late that year, and about the middle of Lent, Eric Burnell was ordered to the seaside. His parents went with him, and the Enderby twins were also of the party;—at first only Dolly was invited for a fortnight's visit, but as she steadily declined to leave her sister, Eric, after a little sulking, asked them both to come. Colonel Enderby went down to Southpool just before Easter, to fetch them home again, and Judy drove him to the station in the pony-cart. When she came back, Geoff, who had arrived the previous day, was in the stable-yard, leaning up against the wall and looking thoroughly unhappy. He took no notice while she and Tom, the stable-boy, unharnessed Snowflake;

but when that work was over, and the usual bits of sugar had been given to the pet, the girl went up to him at once.

"Geoff, what is the matter?" she began.

For a wonder Geoffrey answered roughly. "Nothing—nothing to *you*, at any rate."

Judith pulled a bit of mortar from the wall, and began to crumble it between her fingers. "I wish you would tell me, old boy," she said wistfully, after a little pause. "Isn't it anything I could help you in?"

"Well, can you? How much money have you got?"

"Thirty shillings, I believe. Do you want it? You can have it all."

"Thanks," said Geoffrey languidly, "but as I want ten pounds, I am afraid it wouldn't be much use."

"Ten pounds! O Geoff! have you been getting into debt?"

"Don't jaw, Miss Judy; I can't stand it."

"Oh no! but will you tell me how it happened?"

It was not an uncommon story that he had to tell. At Sunbury he had been thrown with older and more extravagant young men, and in his desire to do what they thought the proper thing, had spent more than his allowance. One of them, called Drayton, kindly lent him ten pounds in the autumn, but at Christmas, Geoff could not bear to mention the subject to his father, and his friend promised to wait until Easter, on condition that he received the money as soon as Enderby went home.

"He wants a post-office order sent off to-day, if possible, or on Saturday at latest," said poor Geoff.

"Shall you have to tell father then?"

"That's it," said Geoff. "That's what I hate. He won't even storm or lecture one, but will just say cuttingly that he had thought I was to be trusted, and is sorry to find himself mistaken. And then he will worry over it alone."

"Is there nothing we can do to spare him?" said Judy. "Unluckily, there is so little time. Dear old fellow, why didn't you tell me this before?"

"Oh, I don't know," he answered awkwardly. "I wanted to, many and many a time, when I was at home before, but though of course it's only natural and one doesn't blame you, things have been so different, and you haven't seemed to care, you know, about the things you used. I couldn't be sure whether you would think it mattered much."

"O Geoffrey, how unkind!" began Judith, but stopt short, her truthful spirit checking the words. There were tears in her eyes as she looked out into the distance, but after a pause she spoke up bravely. "Geoff, I am so sorry. You mean that I have been shutting myself up away from you, just because I was unhappy, and all the time I have been thinking that *you* were hard and cruel, and not seeing that it was my own fault. Any other time, without your telling me, I should have known that you were bothered."

"Never mind," said Geoffrey kindly. "I am glad you know it now."

"I have an idea," said Judith. "Wait until to-night at bedtime, and I will see if it is any good. After tea you are going to ride, aren't you?"

"Yes, I am going to see Harry Grey."

Judith's scheme was spirited and generous. When Geoff started for his evening ride, she ran up to her room, and pulling out her little jewel-drawer and dressing-case, began carefully to examine a quantity of pretty ornaments, which had been either given or left to her by aunts and godmothers. A few more had been her mother's, and putting these aside with Birdie's coral beads and the locket with her own hair that she had given upon the child's last birthday, Miss Judy unceremoniously tilted the rest into a basket, brushing away the tears which had gathered in her eyes, with an impatient exclamation, "What a duffer I am!" and then sat down upon the dressing-table to consider.

Half-way down the village street, next to the "Dog and Partridge" Inn, and almost opposite the blacksmith's, stood the dingy little shop of Bolderson, the working jeweller, and it occurred to Judith that if she took her trinkets there, he might perhaps give sufficient money in exchange to cover Geoffrey's debts. She was a little sorry to part with some of her small treasures, but after all, as she said to herself, she had never really cared for jewellery or dress or any of that nonsense, and the only difficulty was how to sell them secretly. Even heedless Judy realised that grown-up people might object to this proceeding, and she was rather nervous lest she should be seen. A disguise would be the thing, but then came the reflection, that as a gipsy or a beggar-woman she would not be thought likely to have such ornaments in her possession, unless she had stolen them, and it would be highly awkward to be taken up for theft.

After all, who was likely to see her? Rory was spending the evening playing piquet with a sick coachman, the servants were at supper, Geoff well disposed of for some hours, and all the rest away. Judy threw on her hat and necktie with her customary grace, and sallied forth, keeping a keen look-out, lest Mr. Lincoln or any of the gardeners should be coming up the street. Fortune seemed to favour her at first, but just before she reached the shop, she had to pass a knot of noisy men who were standing round the door of the "Dog and Partridge," and as she paused a few yards distant, waiting till they grew a little quieter, her courage oozed away, and she felt shy and frightened, and not at all inclined for what she had to do. Only the thought of Geoff's necessity kept her to the point, and grasping her basket firmly, she was going on again, when a hand upon her shoulder made her start, and a voice, which sounded strangely like her father's, said sternly in her ear, "Judy, what do you mean by loitering *here?*"

It was Geoffrey. His horse had cast a shoe, obliging him to come back to the blacksmith's, and while waiting there and idly looking across the street, he saw a figure that reminded him of Judy. Never thinking that it really was his sister, he was interested simply in the resemblance, until she moved and came more clearly into view, when, recognising her at once, he sprang across the road, and drew her a little way apart. "What are you doing? This is no place for you with all those men about. Tell me what is in that basket?"

"Don't, Geoff!" said his sister; but as he pushed aside the lid and saw the collection of girlish ornaments, the full meaning of her action rushed on him. His face changed quickly. "O Miss Judy, Miss

Judy, this was your idea! I am glad I saw you. It is awfully good of you, but you don't think I am quite so mean as to let you make a sacrifice like that?"

"But do! why shouldn't you? I wish you would," urged Judith with a brighter face than she had shown for weeks. "Is it that you think I shall be sorry for it afterwards? Indeed I shan't. I don't care in the least for looking nice, and even if I did, I should like you to have these all the same. And if they aren't enough," she went on courageously, "(for I daresay jewellers cheat one fearfully in exchanging, and we shouldn't either of us know a bit what these are worth), there is another locket—with pearls—at home. Shall we go in now together, and see what Bolderson will give?"

"As if *anything* would make me sell my sister's jewellery," said Geoff conclusively. "No, no, Miss Judy, you don't know what you are talking of, and it was lucky I was here in time to stop you. I have made up my mind to tell my father, and anyway I couldn't take your things. It isn't that I'm not awfully obliged to you for thinking of it."

"I suppose it's right," said Judith ruefully; "only I would much rather that you would take these. I hope he won't be very angry."

"Even if he is," said Geoff, "I ought to be able to

bear the consequences of such a stupid scrape. Now, go home, and cheer up. It's not your fault, at any rate."

Colonel Enderby received his son's confession very kindly, and lent him the money which was to be repaid by small instalments, and then he sat down and had a little grave conversation with him about his future life. He knew that his boy was to be trusted, and when touched by the depth of his father's confidence Geoff went out of the study, it was not of him that the Colonel sat and pondered, but of Judith's share in the transaction. Hers would be such a noble nature under proper training, and he felt so grievously incompetent to guide it. Aunt Dolly could not often be spared by Major Lennox, and although she frequently asked her niece to visit her, Judy had a great dislike to leaving home. Gradually his thoughts reverted to his stay at Southpool.

One dutiful daughter had seen him off at Norrington, and at his journey's end he was awaited by two rosy little sailor-girls in black serge dresses and straw hats. As he walked with them to the hotel where the Burnells were staying, they told him long and eager stories of their doings and adventures, one of which seemed really to have been exciting. The three children had, as usual, been left upon the shore, Eric lying in a safe and sheltered little nook, while the twins made short excursions among some rocky pinnacles which were quite uncovered at low tide; they were capital climbers, and almost every day they managed to attain a greater height. Eric, who had rather a turn for natural history (which, now that Dolly and Dulcie could find specimens for him, he no longer affected to despise), was on this particular occasion buried in a book on shells, and the little girls had set their minds upon reaching the very highest point of a tall and slippery rock which stood farther out to sea than any they had hitherto attempted. When at last they succeeded, and waved their handkerchiefs to him in triumph, Eric, with a start of horror, was the first to perceive that the tide had turned, and their retreat was quite cut off. A boat was lying on the shore with which it would be easy enough to save them, if any one would come in time, and Eric shouted with his whole strength, hoping that his voice would reach some passer-by along the cliff above. At first there was no answer; the way was lonely, and Eric was beginning to be seriously alarmed, when presently there was a call, and half-way down a path on the cliff, he saw a widow lady who, with her little girl, had arrived the previous day at their hotel. He pointed to the little figures clinging to the rock.

"Don't be frightened," said the lady kindly. "If only they will stay quietly as they are, there is plenty of time. There is a coastguard station down below, and I will give the alarm as quickly as I can."

Help was not long in coming, but the waiting time passed very slowly both to anxious Eric, and to Dolly and Dulcie, who, although they scorned to own it, felt giddy and frightened in their perilous position; and it was a great relief when, manned by two strong coastguards, the boat was rowed up to the rock, and brought them off in safety. Then came a curious recognition: Mr. and Mrs. Burnell came up as they were all discussing the adventure, and discovered in the little girls' preserver, Mrs. Heathcote, the widow of an old friend.

"Wasn't it a good thing she was walking on the cliff," said Dulcie, "or we might both have been drowned? And oh, father, she is very glad that you are coming, for she knew you long ago."

"Now you are romancing," said the Colonel, "for I don't know *any* Mrs. Heathcote."

"Oh, but long ago, before she married; and her name is Dulcie too."

"And she has a little girl called Winnie, the dearest little girl," said Dolly, "and we play together every day."

"DOLLY AND DULCY......... ALTHOUGH THEY SCORNED TO OWN IT, FELT GIDDY AND FRIGHTENED IN THEIR PERILOUS POSITION"
Chap. V.

"I think I know who it must be," he answered.

Yes, except that little namesake daughter now walking by his side, there had been but one Dulcie in his life. How well he remembered her, the tall slim girl of seventeen whom he had loved in early manhood; but she was an heiress, and a warning from her father, who thought the poor young soldier was no match for her, prevented him from knowing how much he was beloved. Perhaps his affection was less deep than hers: at any rate he married, long before Miss Scott could be prevailed on to accept one of the many offers made to her, and in his happiness he had lost sight of his early love. She had not been so happy, but her husband was dead, and now with Winifred she had settled down contentedly. She was naturally much altered. In the calm and stately lady, who met him with the quiet warmth of an old friend, Colonel Enderby could trace little of the laughing Dulcie Scott of old, yet in her presence there came back to him a sense of rest and satisfaction, which had been wanting for the last two years. He was glad to think that Mrs. Burnell told him that Mrs. Heathcote was coming to stay with her in June.

CHAPTER VI.

BABYLAND.

> "She hath her toy,
> Her pretty kingdom. And it is her joy
> To dandle the doll-people, and be kind
> And careful to it, as a child."
> —*Catterina Cornaro.* OWEN MEREDITH.

"RORY, please, will you be very kind?"

Dulcie was the speaker. A pouring wet day, the last but one of the Easter holidays, had driven even Roderick indoors, where he sat with his elbows on the schoolroom table, intent upon his favourite literature, "Lillywhite's Guide to Cricketers," and the twins played quietly together in the Babylanders' special corner of the room, until, after a whispered consultation, they came towards their brother, Dulcie kneeling on a chair which faced him, and Dolly standing by. It was a little confusing to be met by a counter-question.

"Well? Aren't I generally?"

"Oh yes!" acknowledged Dulcie, "but we want you to do something that we think you won't much like."

"Drive on," said Rory, after a little pause in which the children waited for encouragement. "I'm just as likely to say 'yes' if you ask straight out at once as if you were to beat about the bush for half an hour."

"It's about Prince Edward," said Dolly, thus admonished. "We think he ought to go to school — to a public school, if possible, and so, though it is very, *very* hard to part with him," (this was said with genuine sadness), "we should like him to go to Winchester with you. We know we could trust you, and if you wouldn't mind taking care of him, it really will be best."

"Will you, dear Rory?" said Dulcie coaxingly.

Rory lifted his head from his book and looked steadily at his sisters for about a quarter of a minute. "What rot!" he said very distinctly, and then tranquilly returned to an analysis of the Surrey bowling for last year.

Dolly sighed. "Never mind! we must pretend that there isn't a vacancy at present, or that the Usurper" (the usual way of speaking of King George), "won't let him go to any public school in Babyland," she said in an undertone to Dulcie as they went back to the cupboard; but Dulcie answered firmly—

"We must try again. Perhaps Rory will change his mind when he gets sorry to go away."

For Rory was very tenderhearted, and happy as he was at Winchester, he never liked the actual parting from his sisters and his home. This was the time when he was most lavish with his pennies to the exiled Babylanders, and Dulcie calmly traded on his weakness when she put off pressing her request until the following day. Even then it was refused, the palpable absurdity of a boy of his age taking, upon any pretext, a little doll to school, being too much for his manliness; and he dreaded the ridicule attending the discovery of such an act of folly.

Dolly and Dulcie were in bed that night and already very sleepy, when they heard the door pushed softly open. "Don't be frightened; it is I!" said Rory's voice, and in he came, holding something as white as his shirt sleeves in his arms.

"O Rory! what have you got?" they asked, as they sat up in bed with a delightful sensation of excitement, caused by this timely and unexpected interruption to the dulness of going quietly to sleep.

"Nothing, only Trojan," said the boy, putting the ugly

terrier upon Dolly's bed, and seating himself on Dulcie's, which was close beside it. "I brought her in from the stable, because I wanted her to sleep with me this last night, and then I couldn't leave her alone in my room in case she barked, and father or Elizabeth should hear and make a row. It isn't about her I came. Only I find I can manage after all to take Prince Edward with me to-morrow, and if you give him to me now, I will stow him away at once."

"Rory! thank you!" said the twins enthusiastically. "Where shall you put him, do you think?"

"There is a secret drawer in my desk," said Roderick, "meant for money, I suppose, but as I never keep any very long, it won't matter about that. Wait a bit while I fetch the desk, and then you can see for yourselves where he will live."

He went away, and Dolly, diving under her pillow, produced the dark-green box which was the exiles' home: she and Dulcie had it at night by turns. "Perhaps we had better really say good-bye to him ourselves, before Rory comes back," she said, feeling for the Prince's distinguishing knife; and then she held out the little figure to Dulcie, who fondly kissed it and murmured a few parting words, and by the time that Dolly had gone through the same ceremony, Rory

G

returned with his big desk, when lighting a candle, he touched a hidden spring and showed the little drawer where the Prince could lie quite comfortably and safely, and "no one be a bit the wiser," as he consoled himself.

"That is very nice!" said Dolly. "I suppose you won't often be able really to take him up to Doctor for his lessons?"

"Oh no!" said Rory from his heart.

"And he can't have any luggage, can he?"

"It won't be any good to him," said Rory, "but you can put anything there is room for in this drawer."

"A little cotton wool for a pillow would be nice and soft," said Dulcie. "Just give me that box with my necklace from the dressing-table: there is some in that;" and Roderick obligingly waited while his future schoolfellow took an affectionate farewell of his family and friends, gave them wise counsels for their conduct in his absence, and finally retired to his nest of cotton wool. Prince Edward's age was very elastic; the twins agreeing once for all that it was better not to fix it, or he "would always be being too young, or too old, for everything," and thus he easily exchanged the *rôle* of father towards his brothers and sisters, for that of schoolboy being sent to school.

But after Rory had departed with Trojan and his desk, and the little room was again in darkness, Dulcie thought she heard a sob from the sister bed.

"Dolly, are you crying?" she asked very gently.

"No—o," said Dolly slowly; "at least, let us pretend it is the Princess Mabel."

It was not until after the departure of the Prince, that the Babylanders, like the English, became "a nation of shopkeepers." The little Enderbys lived before the present era of expensive toys; but once, when they were ill, a German girl had lent them a beautiful grocer's shop with real glass windows, where jars and canisters with printed labels stood on shelves around, and a counter in the middle held the weights and measures and a shining pair of copper scales. Here for a time Mr. Richardson, the Babylander, drove a thriving trade, but when the twins were strong again, the business had to be disposed of; and the grocer and his family retired into private life. It was Dolly who suggested that, now Prince Edward was away, it would be better fun to leave the royal people alone a little—"they feel his loss so much that they would rather live as quietly as possible"—and set up a big grocer's shop in the palace kitchen, the most convenient place on account of the range of china-shelves upon one side.

The cook supplied them with their stock in trade—a little tea and coffee, currants and raisins, lump sugar and brown sugar, cloves and cinnamon and mace, sago, rice, and tapioca, and long thin pipes of macaroni, which, tied up with cherry-coloured ribbon, looked very effective in a corner. Mr. Richardson found three assistants in his family, his two little sons, of whom Charlie was as good and priggish as his brother James was naughty, and his only daughter Alice, a demure and sweet-faced maiden, who, at the tender age of thirteen, went suddenly into very high prim dresses and white mob-caps, fastened beneath the chin by pretty little bows. Dolly and Dulcie smiled roguishly if any one remarked on Alice's costume, but did *not* reveal the secret that the poor girl had fallen down a precipice—from the top of the babyhouse—and broken off her head, which was only held on to her shoulders henceforth by her quaint attire.

Judith presented her sisters with a little pair of scales, showed them how to make a counter out of a long wooden box, and set out samples of their goods upon it in a collection of round china trays from their sixpenny paintboxes; while many of the servants were kind enough to act as customers upon wet days. Colonel Enderby gave a store of farthings to carry on the business, and often the demand for currants and raisins and lump sugar exceeded the supply. Dolly told Eric all about the shop one day, when he was unusually gracious, even volunteering an inquiry for Prince Edward, of whom he had not heard for weeks.

"We have very good accounts, thank you," said Dolly grandly; "he is at Winchester with Rory."

Eric smiled. "You make-believe he is, I suppose," he answered. "Where do you keep him, really?"

"I mean *really*," answered Dolly. "Dulcie said she thought he ought to go to school, and when I didn't like to part with him, she said that she was sure you would think so too."

Eric took no notice of this weighty argument in favour of the plan. He only said with fervour, "Well! it's awfully good of Rory."

Example is better than precept. Eric listened patiently to the history of the Richardsons, and soon afterwards when Dolly went to Oakleigh, he gave her some neatly-painted placards to hang up on the shop walls. They were advertisements of "Brown and Polson's Corn Flour," "Colman's Mustard," "Thorley's Food for Cattle," "Epps's Cocoa—grateful—comforting," and "When you ask for Glenfield Starch, see that you get it."

Selling groceries grew in time monotonous, so the enterprising Mr. Richardson bought the adjoining property—otherwise the dining-room—and started Alice and Charlie in a china business, a convenient way of disposing of the crockery, which was turned out of the kitchen shelves. This was followed by a jeweller's shop in the bedroom, kept by Ferdinand Fordati and his mother, whose goods were of the paltriest description, consisting mainly of glass beads; and the Cavendish brothers monopolised another branch of industry by becoming chimney-sweeps. The palace chimneys were movable, and made convenient little holes of houses for small families.

It was a great pleasure to the twins when, on the first of June, Mrs Heathcote and Winifred arrived at Oakleigh; and Winnie was quickly initiated into the mysteries of Babyland. Although very shy with grown-up people, she was a charming playmate, and her Southpool experiences gave the nation new ideas.

"Babyland must have a fleet!" she said.

Babyland was very willing, but had neither money, ships, nor seaboard at command, trifling obstacles, however, which were quickly overcome.

"First of all we must have some walnut-shells," said Dolly. "You go and ask for them, Dulcie; I know there are walnuts in the storeroom for dessert—and I will get some bits of calico from the rag-bag."

Dulcie ran down to the study. "Please, father, may we have a lot of walnuts to make ships with?" she said, standing in the doorway; and without looking up from his writing, Colonel Enderby absently replied, "Certainly! as many as you like!" Armed with this generous permission, Dulcie extorted a goodly number from the housekeeper, and returned with them in triumph to the nursery, where Winifred and Dolly were already hard at work cutting three-cornered bits of calico for sails, and sticking them on pins by way of masts. The walnuts required careful cracking, so as not to split them in the wrong direction; but in the course of a few days, two or three dozen boats were fitted out, and ready to start upon a summer's cruise. It was unlucky that just when their preparations were completed, a wet Saturday afternoon prevented the launching of their fleet in the drinking-tub for the cattle in the field; but the twins proposed to Winnie, who was spending the day with them at Woodlands, that rather than postpone the great event, they should adjourn to the bathroom, lock the door to secure themselves from interruption, and turn the big white marble bath into the mimic sea.

It was a very successful play at first. A step-like arrangement of wooden bricks upon the ledge of the bath made a capital grand-stand, whence the Baby-landers watched the ceremony; and there George the Usurper and their Royal Highnesses the Princesses Laura and Mabel met for once in peace and harmony. The flag-ship was the ironclad "Duke Henry," a little, old tin steamer, which together with a duck and drake and magnet had been given to Rory long ago, and Prince Alfred was the Admiral, four of the other boats being named, in compliment to his fraternal feelings, the "Edward," "Laura," "Mabel," and "Hector." Little Prince Hector himself commanded one of the walnut shells. The bath was very deep, and Dolly and Dulcie and Winifred, being small, were naturally obliged to fill it nearly full of water before they could play with it conveniently; and as the boats were most unsteady and occasionally upset, sending their cargoes to the bottom, it followed that in diving after them, the little girls got very wet indeed. They tried to fasten up their sleeves, but the pins had a way of coming out at the critical moment of a plunge.

"What fun it would be," said Dolly, looking damp and happy and excited, as she rescued two of the unlucky ships from their ocean-bed, and swamped

"WHAT FUN IT WOULD BE' SAID DOLLY......'TO PULL THE SHOWER BATH STRING."
Chap. VI.

another pair in the attempt,—" what fun it would be to pull the shower-bath string, and have a regular storm which would send nearly all the boats to the bottom! It would come down just like thunder rain."

"Oh yes," said Dulcie, "and Winnie can knock the coal-box lid to sound like thunder—it *is* tin, isn't it? and there's a looking-glass up there that we can flash about for lightning."

"Are you ready, then?" cried Dolly. "Now! I'm going to pull the string."

"No; wait!" said Dulcie; "the Admiral must come out because of his velvet coat."

It was a tremendous storm and terribly disastrous. Dolly stood upon the edge of the bath to reach the cord, which was supposed to be put carefully beyond the children's fingers; Dulcie bent forward and caught up the black velvet Prince; Winifred was close behind; then down, down came the torrent of water, drenching the three children in an instant. Dolly turned to jump down, but her foot touched the Princess Laura, who tumbled headlong into the sea, and poor Dulcie, trying instinctively to save her, lost her balance, and with a heavy splash followed her royal mistress to the bottom. It was a scene of wild excitement. The pelting shower blinded Dolly as she grasped her sister's clothes, and neither she nor Winnie had the least notion how to stop the downpour. Winifred, who had rushed frantically to the door to shout for help, found the lock too stiff to yield to her tiny fingers, and a little time was lost in struggling with it before the thought occurred to them to ring the bell; her screams, however, had reached a passing housemaid, whose answering call gave the alarm, and a little crowd soon gathered on the landing. Long before they gained an entrance by the key, which Winnie pushed to them beneath the door, Dulcie had scrambled to dry land, shaken and miserable, and with a huge bump rising on her forehead, which had come in contact with the marble of the bath; her little friend was crying out of sympathy, and Dolly shivering with bewilderment and fright.

For once Elizabeth was very angry. The children looked such wretched little objects, that she felt both annoyed by their untidiness and anxious for their health. They would catch their deaths of cold, she said; and unless Miss Winnie's things were taken off and dried directly, she never could go home in them, and she would have to stop in bed while they were being done. Indeed, bed was the best place for all three of them! And regardless of their feelings of disgust and indignation, the culprits were marched off, Colonel Enderby, who had come up to see what was the matter, declining to interfere. But Miss Judy whispered words of comfort. "Pretend you like it, and I will come and play with you," she said; and accordingly when Elizabeth had popped the twins in Dolly's bed, and Winnie Heathcote in the other, Judith intercepted her as she was bringing a hot drink, and took it into them herself, calling it medicine, and suggesting that they should look upon themselves as shipwrecked mariners, and she would be the doctor restoring them to life.

"Isn't there generally an ignorant person in the crowd who lifts up the drowning man by the heels to let the water run out?" said Dolly, who had apparently been studying the directions of the Humane Society at Southpool; and Winnie looked up eagerly at Judy.

"Oh, *do* be the ignorant person, and try on me," she said. "And me!" "And me!" echoed two other little voices.

"What else is there one mustn't do?" said Dolly, when, amid shouts of laughter, Judy had in turn held up each pair of rosy little feet, the long hair of the victim sweeping down upon the bed. Dolly was alluding not to general conduct, but to treatment of the drowned.

"You mustn't rock the body violently to and fro," quoted Dulcie: and accordingly that process too was gone through, the Princess Laura, who in her clinging pale grey dress presented a deplorable appearance, coming in for a share of this energetic kindness.

It was at this moment that Colonel Enderby looked in. "Is this *supposed* to be a punishment?" he said.

"It is making the best of a bad business," said Dolly saucily, leaning her head against him; and shortly afterward Elizabeth appeared in a relenting mood, bringing Winnie's clothes, and followed by Letty with the twins' white evening frocks. "As they seemed none the worse for their adventure, they might get up again," said Nurse, Judy shrewdly surmising that it would have been more trouble for so many of them to have tea in bed. Only the Princess Laura, who had no change of raiment, was supposed to go to sleep, until Winifred, declaring that "Mother did dress dolls so beautifully," insisted upon carrying her off with her to Oakleigh, whence she was returned in a few days, a perfect triumph of artistic skill. In those days there was a favourite photograph of the Princess Mary of Cambridge in a black silk dress with little flounces to the waist; and Laura's costume was a copy, with no fewer than nine flounces, wonderful for a princess who was not four inches high! She had also a velvet porkpie hat with a scarlet feather, and all her clothes took off and on! It was worth a ducking, Dulcie thought.

CHAPTER VII.

THE SECOND MRS. ENDERBY.

> "He might perhaps have blamed them, but his wife
> Never failed to take the children's part:
>   She would stay him with her pleading tone
>   Saying she would strive, and strive alone,
> Till she gained each little wayward heart."
>   —*A New Mother.*   ADELAIDE A. PROCTOR.

"MISS JUDY, you have been writing long enough," said Colonel Enderby, entering the study on a lovely summer afternoon when his daughter was diligently copying. "Besides, you should be ready to receive our guests, and they may be here directly."

Judy looked up with a smile.

"Oh, what a bore! when I am so nearly at the end of a chapter. There is no hurry, is there? I have nothing to do but to get the ink off my fingers, and salts of lemon does that at once."

"And what about your dress and hair?"

"My frock was clean this morning," returned Judy, surveying her crumpled frills complacently, "and that is only the mark of Pepper's paw when he jumped on me at lunch. My hair" (springing up and glancing in a looking-glass), "yes, it isn't very tidy. Perhaps I might as well run up and give it a brush."

"You had better ask Elizabeth to replait it, and if you have not another washing-dress, put on the one you wear on Sundays."

"I will, if you like," said Judy, "but it seems such a fuss about nothing, only for Mrs. Heathcote. Mrs. Burnell has seen me often enough like this."

"Never mind!" he answered, smiling. "I want you to look nice to-day, and they have not been our visitors before. We must do everything in our power to make such kind friends welcome."

"Yes," said puzzled Judith, and she walked up slowly to her room. For more than a month Mrs. Heathcote had been staying at Oakleigh, and gossip speedily began to couple her name with Colonel Enderby, who had not only dined there pretty often, but went frequently to call. Through the servants, one or two significant remarks reached Judith's ears, and were received by her contemptuously. Her father's second marriage seemed too wild and dreadful an idea even to be thought of, and the marked improvement in his spirits, on which people commented, she quietly assigned to her own influence. And yet a vague distrust and jealousy made her hold aloof from Mrs. Heathcote, whose charm of manner gained the hearts of all the rest: instead of being won to confidence by her kindly interest, Judith felt always shy and awkward and uncouth beside her, and shrank from the disagreeable sensation of a contrast which produced such envious dissatisfaction with herself. And to-day her father's manner troubled her. He surveyed her critically, and as if he were not altogether pleased with the effect, even when she came down in her Sunday frock; and Judy did not like to be puzzled. She felt unreasonably cross and disinclined to do the honours of the tea-table, while Mrs. Burnell leant back in an easy-chair in the shade of the friendly beech-tree, talking confidentially to Dolly about Eric's health; and Dulcie and little Winnie handed cups, and cake, and bread-and-butter with a pretty grace, contrasting favourably with the gloomy silence with which Judith was presiding, standing awkwardly before the tray, and answering Mrs. Heathcote's occasional remarks as shortly as she dared. When, afterwards, Mrs. Burnell asked to go over the conservatories and a general move was made, the girl seized the opportunity of making her escape, and was no more seen until the guests had departed. Geoff and Rory, however, who had been riding, soon joined them; and there was a merry, rambling inspection of the pets and premises, in the course of which Mrs. Heathcote found herself alone with Dulcie on the lawn. Between these two there had sprung up an instinctive sympathy, and the child's face lighted up with gladness when, declaring she was tired, Mrs. Heathcote went back into the arbour, and sitting down, took Dulcie on her knee.

"You love me a little, don't you, dear?" she asked her gently; "and you are very good to Winifred, I know;" to which Dulcie answered with a mute caress.

After a while Mrs. Heathcote unfastened from her neck a gold locket with the word "Dulcie" on it in raised letters, and put it on the little girl.

"I feel as if your being my little namesake gave us a peculiar right to one another, and I want you to keep this locket always, in remembrance of to-day. The hair is Winnie's, so you can leave it as it is."

"Oh, thank you! it is lovely!" said Dulcie ecstatically, "and may Dolly wear it too, sometimes? We always have everything together."

"Dolly shall have another with her own name: I

will give it," said Colonel Enderby rashly, who had come up unobserved behind them. "Now you had better run away and tell her. She is near the kitchen garden, I believe."

Less than an hour later, Colonel Enderby, returning from the gate where he had bade the visitors good-bye, saw Judith in the distance, and called to her. She came reluctantly, knowing that her rudeness had displeased him; but he made no allusion to it, and they turned together to a sheltered alley, called by the children the "back walk."

"I was just going to look for you," he said, and although he hesitated, and seemed, if such a thing were possible to him, almost *shy*, she could not help being struck by the brightness of his face. "My dear, I have something to tell you which, I hope, you will see is for the happiness of us all. I am going to be married. Mrs. Heathcote has promised to be my wife."

"O father!" burst from Judy in accents of such passionate reproach, that he was positively startled.

He put his arm gently round her, and they sat down on an iron seat close by.

"No doubt it will be a trial to you at first," he said affectionately. "My wild girl has been unaccustomed to authority, but, indeed, I can assure you that no one could be kinder or more gentle than *she* will be. I am not going to persuade you that, like many second marriages, this step is taken solely for my children's good,—I love her far too well for that—but, believe me, my own hopes and happiness would have been sacrificed, had I not seen in her one who will as far as possible be like a mother to you all."

After that first startled exclamation Miss Judy set her face impassively. "I don't much like Mrs. Heathcote," she said perversely. "If it had to be, I wish it had been some one else."

Her father sighed. Judith was so dear to him that, apart from his anxiety for the future, he would have rejoiced in a more sympathetic reception of his news. "Wait until you know her better, and then I think you will change your mind," he said with an effort to speak kindly. But she edged herself away from him.

"Do the others know?" she said.

"Not yet; I shall tell Geoff directly, and Rory and the children afterwards. Don't speak of it to them. I wished to tell you each myself; you first, Miss Judy, because I thought you would have cared so much about my happiness."

"I didn't know you were unhappy before," returned

Judith, moving restlessly, as if she longed to get away; and when her father left her and went back into the house, she rushed off to the churchyard and flung herself weeping, upon her mother's grave. There was a sound of music in the distance, some one practising the organ in the church, but Judy paid no heed to outward things, in the sense of lonely desolation which swept over her as she called out "Mother, mother!" or her little sister's name. Poor child! her tears were very bitter, and she hardly understood the nature of her grief. She felt angry, and sorry, and naughty, and neglected all at once, and there seemed no comfort anywhere. It was not the dread of the stepmother of fairy tales who would rule her harshly, or perhaps be positively unkind; Miss Judy was too old for such a notion; but beyond the natural pang of seeing a stranger in her mother's place, there was the downfall of her hopes and visions of being the future consolation of her father's life. How bright he looked at teatime as he stood talking in the arbour! This new wife would teach him to forget his sorrows, and win the hearts of her younger stepchildren with her gracious ways. Judith, who said she did not like her, did full justice to the fascination to which she was determined not to yield, and there was much of the same charm in

"AND FLUNG HERSELF WEEPING UPON HER MOTHER'S GRAVE"

Chap: VI

Winifred, who, while her mother reigned instead of Judy's mother, would be the household's darling, just as Birdie used to be. The twins, particularly Dulcie, already seemed to look upon her as a sister, and in imagination Judith saw them happy and forgetful of her absence while she was miserable at school, with the prospect of the very holidays spoilt by the knowledge of the changes in her home.

She never knew how long she stayed there. Her tears had nearly spent themselves, and she was weary and exhausted, when she felt a cold touch on her forehead, and looking up, met the beautiful brown eyes of Mr. Lincoln's dog. It was a comfort to throw her arms around her and bury her wet face in Lassie's silky hair; and in a little while she dried her eyes, sat up, and in order to regain composure, even tried to whistle a few bars: the result was hardly satisfactory, but the effort did her good. She was not sorry for the distraction when Lassie's master came in sight, and without appearing to notice her tear-stained cheeks, abruptly said—

"I told Dulcie I would let her know if I saw the hare again in that field below. It is there this evening; would you like to look?"

"I should," said Judy, jumping up.

She had never before talked much with Mr. Lincoln,

and rather laughed at Dulcie for her fervent admiration, in which, owing to his being Eric's tutor for two afternoons a week and finding favour in his eyes, Dolly was disposed to join. As they walked to the neighbouring field, he began to question her about the natural history of the district, and Judy liked to tell him of the birds and flowers and butterflies they had observed. Her spirits rose, her trembling voice grew steadier, and although there was still that underlying sense of wrong and misery, she couldn't help being a little interested in her new friend. It was not until after they had seen the hare, and were back again in the churchyard, that he seemed to notice her tears.

"And now, if you are in any scrape, perhaps I could help you to get out of it," he said suddenly, looking at her with kindly eyes. "Wouldn't you like to tell me all about your trouble?"

"Yes, I should—*awfully*," said Judith, answering his look with honest frankness, "but I don't think I ought. It isn't a scrape exactly; at least it isn't one of my own making; and it concerns some other people too. I wonder if there would be any harm in telling you?" she added wistfully; "it is rather a secret, I am afraid."

"It is better to keep on the safe side then, isn't it?" said the curate, perceiving that her grief had a deeper source than childish naughtiness, and from the rumours he had heard of late, making a prompt guess at the truth. After a pause, during which Miss Judy had some difficulty in keeping back fresh tears, he began again—

"If you were abroad, you would find the church doors always open, and see people going into them with their troubles and telling them there. Would you like to go into church now? The door is open, for I was playing on the organ a little while ago."

"I should like you to go on playing," said Judy shyly.

That was not exactly what he wished her to respond, but he answered readily—

"Oh yes, if I can find the boy to blow for me: he is one of the choristers, and I left him overhauling the music books for a practice later on."

Miss Judy crept into a pew and knelt there: she was not praying or even thinking consciously, but as she listened to the solemn tones of the organ, she felt soothed and comforted, and the Saviour's figure in the east window seemed stretching out His arms as if saying—"Come unto Me, and I will give you rest."

Would she resist that loving invitation, or answer it by laying down her hard rebellious thoughts? At length the music ceased, and at a sign from Mr. Lincoln, she followed him into the open air.

"What made you come and speak to me?" she asked with blunt frankness. "I thought you hated making friends with people, and at home we always call you 'the shy curate,' or 'Dulcie's friend.'"

"I hope I'm not too shy to try and comfort those who want me," he answered gravely, "but it *is* a check to usefulness, and though I don't suppose you meant it, that was a just rebuke."

Then Judith being too confused to utter a disclaimer, they crossed the churchyard and the lane in silence, till at the small gate leading to the Woodlands garden, Mr. Lincoln held out his hand.

"Good-bye," he said with one of his rare smiles, "and remember that in future you are *not* to call me only 'Dulcie's friend.' I am going to be yours as well."

"All right, thank you," said Judy, looking up. "Dulcie won't mind a bit. She is used to sharing things, you know, because of Dolly."

The girl went home in a curious mood, half softened half rebellious; and had there been any one to understand her, she might easily have been beguiled from her foolish notion of hostility towards Mrs. Heathcote. But, alas!

she met with little sympathy. Geoffrey, who certainly disliked the idea of his father's second marriage on his own account, was old and sensible enough to see that it would be a good thing for his sisters; Rory really didn't care; and the twins were charmed with the prospect of having Winifred to live with them. The engagement was to be a very short one.

"Do you mean to say you really like it—all of you?" said Eric in amazement, the first time Dolly went to see him afterwards.

"Not Judy," Dolly said.

"I should think not!" Eric answered. "Tell her from me that I should hate it too."

Thus matters stood, when the wedding-day was fixed for the first week in September, and soon after a letter came from Mrs. Heathcote, who had gone to Edinburgh, saying that, as the marriage was to take place there, a friend of hers had offered to put up Judith and the boys, if their father chose them to be present. He told them of the invitation, and left it to themselves to accept it or decline. Geoff not only meant to go, but brought his shyer brother to the same decision: their father evidently wished it, and they had no right to thwart him: but with his sister he was not conciliatory. Her opposition angered him: he thought it childish and unreasonable, and besides, it kept alive his own dislike to seeing another in his mother's place, which he was trying hard to conquer. With a little coaxing she would gladly have recalled her hasty declaration, that nothing should induce her to go to the wedding, but Geoff's righteous indignation, when he thought it was a fixed resolve, drove her into standing by the colours she had recklessly assumed. "In fact, you disapprove so thoroughly of the whole proceeding, that you really cannot countenance it with your presence," said Geoff sarcastically, while Rory laughed outright.

If Miss Judy hoped to be persuaded to change her resolution, she was disappointed, and although her father might regret her absence, he was evidently pleased by her suggestion that the twins should take her place. It would be a great delight to Winifred, who was not coming to Woodlands until Colonel and Mrs. Enderby returned, early in October, from their wedding tour. Judy felt dreary and aggrieved when the party set out joyously for Edinburgh, where Major and Mrs. Lennox were to meet them; and her father's few grave tender words at parting would have been too much for her composure, had not pride come to her aid, and prevented her from showing how she longed for an assurance that this new marriage would not make him love her less.

Poor Queen Judith! she felt as if a usurper were coming to her kingdom, and made a valiant effort to keep the hearts of the few subjects who were left within her power. The boys had gone back to their studies, but Dolly and Dulcie, on their return from Scotland, were enchanted to find their elder sister so bright and loving and considerate: she gave handsome presents to the Babylanders, and actually cooked the wedding-breakfast when, in humble imitation of their seniors, the pretty Princess Laura married Prince Lionel-Leopold, and went to live with him in the old French-plum box. She even coaxed Eric Burnell into writing a comic history of the kingdom as an amusement for wet weather, and really made him rather interested in that ideal land. For fine days there was now another occupation. Long ago, at Eric's instigation, Mr. Burnell had offered Rory the right of fishing in his pond, which, to his surprise, the boy refused, stammering, colouring, and then frankly owning his secret expeditions. Mr. Burnell received the avowal kindly, but did not repeat his offer until the summer holidays, when it was eagerly and gratefully accepted, and Miss Judy suggested that if Eric's couch were drawn close to the water, she saw no reason why he should not hold a rod: some one else could play and land the fish for him. And thus the days slipped by before the children had done half they wished to do.

It was on a bright October evening that the second Mrs. Enderby came to her new home, where she was warmly greeted on the threshold by the little twins, while Judith stood there behind them, very neat and tidy, but very grave and cold: nor was there any gladness in her manner as she returned her father's kiss. She had taken her resolution that, while obeying all positive commands and suffering few complaints to be made against her, she would present a steady front of cold dislike to the stepmother, whose position she resented, and show her that in every way she thought her an intruder in their happy home. At any rate, thought Judith, I will keep my brothers and sisters for my own! and Geoff and Roderick, as they read the cheery, loving letters which came so frequently just now, had no suspicion of the tears she shed while writing them. Neither did the twins discover that the curious fact, that they were always engaged to Judith for some special entertainment whenever Mrs. Enderby was likely to have leisure to attend to them, was the result of a careful system, though they were often sorry that these pleasures were such as Winnie's different training unfitted her to join : she was not nearly as daring or surefooted as the little Enderbys. So weeks went on, Judy's active mind finding occupation in methodical resistance; and although at times her conscience strove to speak, she silenced it with the assurance that her father had deceived her, pretending to care so much for her society, while he was planning all the time to send her off to school, out of the way of this woman whom he loved.

And meanwhile, Mrs. Enderby's gentleness and patience never failed. Though hurt and grieved beyond measure by Miss Judy's naughtiness, her chief anxiety was to spare her husband the knowledge of its full extent, often fearing even to speak to her before him, lest he should be struck by the rude indifference of her tone.

She was standing in the drawing-room window, one December day, thinking sadly of these things, when Colonel Enderby came in. "Where are the girls?" he said, "I met Winnie in the garden looking very disconsolate, and she told me that the others had gone out."

Mrs. Enderby smiled. "Poor Winnie! she was anxious to go with them, but it was for a long ramble in search of hollyberries, and I knew she could not walk so far. Geoffrey, I want to talk to you of Judith: we must not let her go to school. I have just been hearing how much she dreads it: Dolly says she cannot bear the least allusion to it, and now that I am here, why should she go? You know you were only sending her because she is too old to run wild in her own fashion, and besides, if once she leaves us, how can I ever gain her love?"

And thus it happened, the next morning after breakfast, that Colonel Enderby sought his daughter in the garden. He felt hopeful for the future, for surely in her gratitude at hearing to whose pleadings she owed the fulfilment of her wish to stay at home, Miss Judy would be softened into penitence, and listen with compunction to his regrets that her stepmother had been treated with so little attention and respect. Great therefore was his disappointment, when, as she grasped his meaning, Judy interrupted in a cold, hard tone—

"But I would rather go to school, *much* rather, thank you. I know I did not like it once, but that was long ago, when home was different. If I am here in the boys' holidays, that is all that matters now."

He was too hurt and indignant to answer her; and with a sudden sinking of the heart, Miss Judy remembered that summer day when, in telling her of his intended marriage, he had put his arm round her and spoken tenderly. Now, with one look of grave displeasure, he walked away.

But she did not rush to the churchyard this time. Conscience spoke too loudly to allow her to fling herself in sorrow on her mother's grave, while between her and her father rose a barrier caused by conduct which that gentle mother would have been the very first most sternly to condemn: little Barbara, even, would have looked on in astonishment. Ah! this was the worst loneliness, the most real separation! But just at that moment there was a footstep on the gravel, and she brushed away her gathering tears as a young gardener approached.

"Miss Judy, did you know as the hounds were to meet to-day at Beekham Corner, and draw Holme Wood? With the wind in this quarter they'll most like run over the moor over here, and you might see them if you liked."

Judy looked up in great excitement. Norrington was quite beyond the reach of ordinary meets, but once or twice a year, under favourable circumstances, a glimpse of the hunt was possible, and there was nothing that the children more enjoyed. This was an unusual opportunity; Miss Gresley had a cold which kept her in her lodgings and caused an unexpected holiday, and Judith was only sorry that, as Dolly and Dulcie had gone with Mrs. Enderby to Milborough, they could not share the treat. She dashed into the stables, and both Tom and the coachman being out, she and the young gardener began rapidly to put Snowflake in the pony-cart. Joe, who was unaccustomed to the business, was not quite so quick as Tom, and Judy's impatience would not suffer her to wait.

"It is sure to be all right," she said in answer to some doubt about the harness, and before he could stop her, she had jumped in with a merry nod of thanks, and was off down the avenue, after a narrow shave of the stable gatepost.

But at the lodge there was an interruption. As she pulled up for the gate to be opened, a little dark-eyed girl, with long fair curls and rosy cheeks, sprang forward.

"O Judy! where are you going? Take me, too."

It was the hardest part of Judy's self-appointed task to steel herself against Winifred; and in spite of her harshness, whenever the child attempted to touch one of Birdie's treasures, or petted Pepper or Jessie-Tibbie-Ruth, Winnie had taken a strong fancy to the tall bright girl to whom Dolly and Dulcie looked up so admiringly. Judy's face now softened into tenderness at the coaxing voice: she was beginning to realise that she loved the child dearly.

"Come then," she said, holding out a hand, "but we must leave a message for your mother. Mrs. Johnson," turning to the woman at the lodge, "will you say that we have gone to look for the hounds on Norton Moor? and can you lend us a shawl or cloak for Winifred?"

The day was clear and bright, and as Judith drove through the delicious frosty air, her mental mists and fogs seemed also to disperse. Even in the bustle and excitement of the start, her father's look had never ceased to haunt her, and yet her jealous heart found comfort in its very sorrow. If he did not care he would not have been so grieved, and now that she had time to think of it, she was touched, too, by her stepmother's proposal that she should stay at home. Judy began to be very much ashamed, as she contrasted this magnanimity with her own misconduct; and since her ungracious reception of the offer made it impossible to re-open the subject, she determined to go cheerfully to Brighton and work hard there for one quarter, and then acknowledge to her father how she loved him and her home, and beg never, never to be sent away again. It was less pleasant to resolve upon the frank apology and immediate change of manner towards Mrs. Enderby, which alone could win her his forgiveness, and as Winnie broke in on these reflections with some eager question, the girl put by her troubles, and yielded to the inspiriting influence of the day and scene.

At length they came across a boy who told them that Holme Wood had been drawn blank, and that the hounds were now on their way to another covert, reached easily by going through some fields and skirting a corner of the moor; and Judy touched up Snowflake, who, from want of exercise of late, was rather fresh, and willingly responded to the call. In a little while there was a distant view of scarlet coats, on which they gradually gained, and presently the pony saw them too, and pricking up his ears, began to pull so that Judith could hardly hold him. She did not know that his former owner was a boy who hunted regularly, and never dreamt that she was running into danger; but as they drew nearer, the familiar music of the huntsman's horn brought back old recollections, and so excited him that, forgetting the light little cart behind, he dashed along at a terrific rate, while Judy, who now knew she could not stop him, did her best to guide his course. Then came a crack, as something gave way in the harness, which put him utterly beyond control, and as he swerved sharply to the right,

Miss Judy's very lips grew white, as a murmur rose to them—"The gravel pits!"

There they lay, straight between them and the red-coats which were Snowflake's lodestar, and Judith might well shudder as every moment brought them nearer the edge of the great excavations, where she and Geoff had spent a merry day last summer, hunting for fossils among the heaps of stones. How little they then thought that this was where she might die!

Miss Judy felt so helpless, so powerless to save, as she threw a supporting arm round Winifred, who, for some time past, had been clinging in speechless terror to her dress, till, by a sudden inspiration, there flashed into her mind a story that her father told, of how, on a similar occasion, a young mother had saved her little son at the cost of her own life. Clasping him tightly to her breast, she had thrown herself out backwards, and the child was found unhurt on her dead body, which had shielded him from even being bruised or shaken by the fall. A strange light came into Judith's face. She had no thought of heroism: it was only her old loving and protecting instinct towards the little ones.

"Come, darling, come!" she said, and dropping the reins, she turned to Winnie, whom she folded in a close embrace, pressing the little face against her bosom. There was no time for prayer, but as she stood up and pulled herself together for the effort, there came, as in a vision, the recollection of the Saviour's pitying figure in the window in the church, and it seemed as if that fatal spring would take her to those Everlasting Arms.

Her own little room, with the blinds drawn down to prevent the wintry rays of sunshine from giving too much light, and an unfamiliar table with glasses and medicine bottles put close up to the bed—that was the next thing Judith was conscious of, as she opened her eyes one afternoon, feeling she was awaking from a long and troubled dream.

Was she ill? had she slept late? what had happened? But the effort to move brought on a sickening sense of pain and languor, and a bewildering remembrance of her drive came over her as she felt herself sinking back into the horrible darkness from which she had escaped. Instantly, however, there was a strong arm round her, and her stepmother's voice said, oh! so tenderly—

"Drink this, dear child," and Judy struggled to obey, and drank the cordial, and after a little interval of faintness, she opened her grey eyes again with an imploring look, which was understood and answered.

"HER OWN LITTLE ROOM WITH THE BLINDS DRAWN DOWN"
Chap VI

"Winifred is safe," said Mrs. Enderby.

There was a silence of intense thanksgiving before Judy spoke.

"Snowflake?" she questioned.

"Poor Snowflake! He did not suffer long. He was found quite dead at the bottom of the gravel-pits. You remember, Judy? you and Winnie must have jumped out together, and you must have fallen underneath, for she was lying upon the top of you, unhurt."

"I know," said Judith quietly.

She was too exhausted to say more, nor had she any idea how long she had been ill, nor of the great anxiety about her which had prevailed. Some one had seen the accident, and recognised the children. Winnie begged to be taken home, but Judith lay insensible and continued to do so throughout the drive, hovering for days thereafter between life and death: concussion of the brain, said Dr. Grey, and probably there were other injuries. But at length the crisis was past, and a few hours before this awakening to full consciousness, there had been a gleam of recognition of the watchers round her bed before she sank into a peaceful sleep. Henceforth her recovery was steady, and, one by one, visitors were admitted to her room. Major and Mrs. Lennox, Geoff, and Rory had assembled for the

Christmas Day that passed so anxiously, and Judith might well be touched by all the tokens of the love surrounding her; her father's thankfulness would be to her a life-long memory. Of course she had much to suffer. The shock to her nerves had been so great that the least noise or motion brought on actual pain, and all excitement was carefully avoided. There were hours when she lay quite still, thinking of many things, while her stepmother kept her quiet watch beside the fire, and Judy learnt to prize her thoughtful tenderness and gentle voice even more than her beloved Aunt Dolly's visits. But as she grew stronger, Mrs. Enderby was less and less with her. Whenever the invalid appeared at all disposed to talk, her favourite nurse would go away and send some one in her place—Mrs. Lennox, or the twins, or Geoff, or Rory, or Elizabeth—it did not seem to matter *whom*, so long as it was not herself; and a burden of deferred confession lay on Judy's soul.

"Are you going away? Are you busy?" she said at last, one day when Mrs. Enderby had risen and was silently attending to her comfort, preparatory to absence from the room; and in spite of its crossness, there was something so wistful in the tone that her stepmother came and stood beside her.

"Yes, dear, unless there is anything you want. I

was going to ask your aunt to come and sit with you."

"I don't want *anything*, I want *you*," Miss Judy said expressively, "and you never seem to have time to stay with me now. You are always sending some one else instead, and they shake the room, or talk too loud, or worry me. It is not a bit the same," she added discontentedly.

She was not prepared for the glad and tender smile that greeted this avowal.

"O Judy, dear! do you mean this? Do you like to have me with you? I have left you whenever you were well enough to do without me, because, knowing how you always avoided me before, I thought perhaps you still disliked my presence. Are your really learning to care for me a little bit at last?"

Was this her grave, calm stepmother who was so agitated? Miss Judy stretched out her arms and threw them round her.

"I have *always* cared for you, really, I think," she said, as well as she could speak for tears, "only I was cross and jealous, and could not bear that father should love you best. Oh, please, forgive me: it shall be different now. Geoff and Rory and the twins all say that home is happier than it has been for years, and

I was sorry even before I thought I had to die. Now every time you look so tired, and worn, and ill with nursing me, I am, oh! much sorrier, and I am so glad to be allowed to try again. It is like a new life given to me to do better with. Will you help me with it, please? I want it to be unlike the old one in almost everything."

"My darling, yes," she answered tenderly. "Have I not Winnie's escape to be thankful for? and we will try together to show our gratitude to God 'not only with our lips, but in our lives; by giving up ourselves to His service, and by walking before Him in holiness and righteousness all our days.'"

"'Through Jesus Christ our Lord, Amen,'" said Judith softly, and there was solemn silence for a while.

THE END.

LONDON: WELLS GARDNER, DARTON, AND CO., PATERNOSTER BUILDINGS.